☆ Daytime Dramas ☆

Sizzling soap operas have given many of today's movie and TV actors their first real break. Catch up with the young soap stars who are on their way to superstardom!

- ☆ **Jonathan Jackson**, Lucky Spencer on *General Hospital*, is also a singer and songwriter.
- ☆ **Adrienne Frantz**, Amber Moore on *The Bold and the Beautiful*, has acted in several independent films.
- ☆ **Jensen Ackles**, Eric Brady on *Days of Our Lives*, won the *Soap Opera Digest* Award for Outstanding Male Newcomer after only four months on the job!

Packed with photos and the ultimate soap opera trivia quiz, you can find all the info on the hottest soap stars on daytime in . . .

☆ Sizzlin' Soap Stars ☆

Look for other celebrity biographies from
Archway Paperbacks

98 Degrees: And Rising to the Top! by Nancy Krulik
Backstreet Boys★Aaron Carter by Matt Netter
Five by Matt Netter
Hanson: MMMBop to the Top by Jill Matthews
Isaac Hanson: Totally Ike! by Nancy Krulik
Taylor Hanson: Totally Taylor! by Nancy Krulik
Zac Hanson: Totally Zac! by Matt Netter
Hanson: The Ultimate Trivia Book! by Matt Netter
Jewel: Pieces of a Dream by Kristen Kemp
Jonathan Taylor Thomas: Totally JTT! by Michael-Anne Johns
Leonardo DiCaprio: A Biography by Nancy Krulik
Pop Quiz: Leonardo DiCaprio by Nancy Krulik
Matt Damon: A Biography by Maxine Diamond with Harriet Hemmings
Most Wanted: Holiday Hunks
Most Wanted: Hunks and Kisses
'N Sync: Tearin' Up the Charts by Matt Netter
'N Sync with JC by Nancy Krulik
'N Sync with Justin by Matt Netter
Pop Quiz by Nancy Krulik
Prince William: The Boy Who Will Be King by Randi Reisfeld
Sizzlin' Soap Stars by Nancy Krulik
Will Power!: A Biography of Will Smith by Jan Berenson

For orders other than by individual consumers, Pocket Books grants a discount on the purchase of **10 or more** copies of single titles for special markets or premium use. For further details, please write to the Vice-President of Special Markets, Pocket Books, 1633 Broadway, New York, NY 10019-6785, 8th Floor.

For information on how individual consumers can place orders, please write to Mail Order Department, Simon & Schuster Inc., 200 Old Tappan Road, Old Tappan, NJ 07675.

Sizzling Soap Stars

Nancy Krulik

AN ARCHWAY PAPERBACK
Published by POCKET BOOKS
New York London Toronto Sydney Tokyo Singapore

The sale of this book without its cover is unauthorized. If you purchased this book without a cover, you should be aware that it was reported to the publisher as "unsold and destroyed." Neither the author nor the publisher has received payment for the sale of this "stripped book."

AN ARCHWAY PAPERBACK *Original*

An Archway Paperback published by
POCKET BOOKS, a division of Simon & Schuster Inc.
1230 Avenue of the Americas, New York, NY 10020

Copyright © 1999 by Nancy Krulik

Certain quotations in the Jensen Ackles, Tyler Christopher, and Vanessa Marcil chapters first appeared in *Soaps in Depth*.

All rights reserved, including the right to reproduce this book or portions thereof in any form whatsoever. For information address Pocket Books, 1230 Avenue of the Americas, New York, NY 10020

ISBN: 0-671-03287-9

First Archway Paperback printing May 1999

10 9 8 7 6 5 4 3 2 1

AN ARCHWAY PAPERBACK and colophon are registered trademarks of Simon & Schuster Inc.

Cover photo credits: top left, Celebrity Photo; top right, © Jon McKee/Retna; bottom left, © Steve Granitz/Retna; bottom right, © Walter McBride/Retna; center, © Jon McKee/Retna

Printed in the U.S.A.

IL 4+

*For Lisa and Liz,
media mavens, amazing editors,
and good friends*

☆ Contents ☆

Tune in Tomorrow	1
1 Jensen Ackles (Eric Brady, *Days of Our Lives*)	7
2 Steve Burton (Jason Morgan [Quartermaine], *General Hospital*)	20
3 Tyler Christopher (Nikolas Cassidine, *General Hospital*)	31
4 Adrienne Frantz (Ambrosia "Amber" Moore, *The Bold and the Beautiful*)	44
5 Rebecca Herbst (Elizabeth Webber, *General Hospital*)	54

☆ Contents ☆

6 Jonathan Jackson
(Lucky Spencer, *General Hospital*)   65

7 Vanessa Marcil
(ex–Brenda Barrett, *General Hospital*)   79

8 Shemar Moore
(Malcolm Winters, *The Young and the Restless*)   97

9 Alison Sweeney
(Sami Brady, *Days of Our Lives*)   107

10 Erin Torpey
(Jessica Buchanan, *One Life to Live*)   116

11 Jacob Young
(Rick Forrester, *The Bold and the Beautiful*)   127

12 The Ultimate Soap Opera Trivia Quiz   137

Sizzling Soap Stars

Tune in Tomorrow . . .

☆ Do you find yourself constantly searching the Internet for the spoilers (hints of the things coming up next week) on your favorite soap?

☆ Have you ever looked on a map to see if there really are such places as Bay City, Port Charles, Genoa City, or Oakdale?

☆ Is your family room overloaded with VCR tapes of episodes of your favorite soap that you haven't had a chance to watch yet?

☆ Do you ever pretend to be sick on a school day just so you can stay home and watch your favorite soap characters get married?

☆ Do you really believe that people can have evil twins they never knew about?

☆ Does it seem normal to you when a skinny little six-year-old goes off to boarding school and returns two years later—as a really hunky eighteen-year-old?

If you were able to answer yes to two or more of these questions, consider yourself a certified soap opera addict! But don't feel bad—you are one of millions. Soap fans can be found all over the world. Several celebrities proudly count themselves among that group—Elizabeth Taylor, Rosie O'Donnell, Little Richard, and LeAnn Rimes have all guest-starred on their favorite soaps.

A Quick Flashback

People have been telling each other serialized stories for centuries. (Hey, people today still call their favorite soaps "my stories," right?) In the days before radio, TV, or even electric lights, authors wrote out their stories and published them as serials in magazines. Readers had to wait a whole month between issues, which meant it was a long time before they could find out if the villain had succeeded, or if the young lovers from different social stations would marry.

In the 1930s and '40s—the golden age of radio—soaps were a staple for the national listening audience. In fact, it was on radio that daytime dramas first began to be called soap operas. They were given the nickname because the commercial sponsors were usually soap companies. Several of those early radio soap operas made the move from radio to TV in the 1950s, but today, only *The Guiding Light* is still on the air.

Most people these days watch their daytime shows on TV—but as always, the soaps are keeping up with the latest technological trends. Internet soaps like *East Village* are recording more and more website hits every week.

Soaps Are Where the Stars Shine

Because TV soap operas air every weekday, people really get to know the characters. They laugh with them, cry with them, love them, and *hate* them. Many of the soap world's best villains claim that a few ferocious fans confuse them with their characters. These actors have been scolded, screamed at, and (in extreme cases) even hit for the actions their characters have taken. Of course that's just a few wild fans. For the most part, soap fans are the best there are. Alison Sweeney, who plays *Days of Our Lives*'s difficult diva, Sami, should know. "Most people I meet realize Sami is a character," she says. "They're very nice."

All daytime actors agree that there are no fans like soap fans. Daytime drama fans are known for holding huge conventions and traveling all over the world to meet their favorite actors. And for a performer, having demonstrative, adoring fans who appreciate your work is what it's all about.

There's no professional training ground quite like a soap opera set. No other medium allows performers to develop their characters quite so completely. And having pages and pages of lines to memorize every night allows actors to exercise their "memory muscles" (as *General Hospital*'s Jonathan Jackson likes to put it). But most importantly, no movie or prime-time show gives actors the chance to become part of their fans' daily lives in quite such an intimate way.

After conquering such a demanding training ground, is it any wonder that many soap opera actors go on to be huge stars after they leave the soap world? Hollywood heavy hitter Demi Moore got her start on *General Hospital* as Jackie Templeton. Oscar winner Marisa Tomei was Marcy Thompson Cushing on *As the World Turns*. And if you're playing Six Degrees of Kevin Bacon some day, keep in mind that the versatile movie star was once *Guiding Light*'s Tim Werner. Even the brightest star in heaven or on earth these days, Leonardo DiCaprio, has a place in soap history. He spent a few months playing an alcoholic teenager on *Santa Barbara*.

Soap stars often leave daytime for careers as TV prime-time players. Famous *Full House*rs John Stamos (Uncle Jesse) and Andrea Barber (Kimmy

Gibler) got their starts on the soaps. John was *General Hospital*'s Blackie Parrish, and Andrea was *Days of Our Lives*'s Carrie Brady. You might also be surprised to find that taking his shirt off for the cameras is nothing new to *Baywatch*'s David Hasselhoff. He was busy doing that back in the early 1970s, when he played sexy Dr. Snapper Foster on *The Young and the Restless*. *General Hospital* alumni Vanessa Marcil (ex-Brenda) and Rena Sofer (ex-Lois) have gone from daytime dramas to nighttime soaps, taking on roles on *Beverly Hills 90210* and *Melrose Place*, respectively.

But not all soap actors have to leave their shows in order to achieve superstardom. Some have achieved huge careers by sticking to their stories. Tony Geary and Genie Francis are forever Luke and Laura in our hearts. And no matter how many TV movies-of-the-week she may make, Susan Lucci will always be Erica Kane. (But will she ever win that Emmy?!)

The New Breed

So which of today's hot young soap stars will go on to accept an Oscar or have top billing in a multimillion-dollar hit? It's hard to say. But there are a few young actors who seem primed for major fame. You know the ones—the kids whose great looks get them noticed, and whose talents keep us coming back for more.

Luckily, you don't have to sit through a commercial or wait for tomorrow's episode to get all the facts on today's sizzling soap studs and starlets. The excitement begins on the very next page!

1

Jensen Ackles

(Eric Brady, *Days of Our Lives*)

Doesn't it seem like Jensen Ackles has it all? He's got good looks, a great-paying job on a hot TV soap, and beautiful women to work with every day. What more could a guy want?

How about some good Texas barbecue?

"The chili and barbecue here [in Los Angeles, where *Days of Our Lives* is filmed] just aren't up to snuff," he complains. "If I go to a restaurant here and I see 'Texas-style,' I know it isn't going to be as good as at home. It never is, but I still have to order it."

Oh well. Guess you can take the boy out of Texas, but you can't take Texas out of the boy. Although Jensen has been in L.A. for a few years now, there are still things about his home state that he misses.

"The biggest differences between Dallas and L.A. are that Dallas is more open, the traffic's not so bad, and of course there's the smog. Dallas is a lot cleaner."

Still, there are things and people you can see in Los Angeles that you won't find anywhere else. For instance, there was that one night when Jensen was shopping in a supermarket and heard an older man singing in the aisles.

"I went up to him, shook his hand, and said, 'I just had to meet you, Mr. Hope,'" Jensen recalls. Bob Hope in a grocery store—now there's something even the Lone Star State can't offer.

Jensen has developed a few ways to keep Texas in his heart and home, however. For starters, both of his roommates are friends from high school, so Texas accents abound in Jensen's L.A. bachelor pad.

"We have Texas flags all over the place," he says, describing the apartment. "We have a nasty case of Texas pride."

And how about the family he left behind? Do the folks in Texas have a nasty case of Jensen pride?

"My older brother [Joshua] is like 'whoopee doo, so you're on a soap,'" Jensen says. "And it's not that big a deal to my [younger] sister [Mackenzie], either."

But Jensen's grandmother is sure glad Jensen's on *Days*. It's her favorite soap. "My grandmother says, 'Now I get to see you every day,'" he laughs.

☆ Sizzlin' Soap Stars ☆

Jensen's Dallas Days

Jensen Ackles was born in Dallas, Texas, but he was raised in Richardson, a Dallas suburb. Unlike other young soap stars, Jensen isn't the first member of his family to get bitten by the acting bug. His father, Alan Ackles, has always been "one of the best-known actors in Dallas," says Jensen's manager, Craig Wargo.

Jensen's dad never hid the tough side of the business from his children. But Jensen also got to see the good side of the acting world.

"My dad's done really well for himself as an actor," Jensen says. "He didn't have a nine-to-five routine like the other fathers, so he came to my football games and spent a lot of time with me and my brother and sister. I see now why my father stuck to it. It's a challenging career, but it also gives you something very valuable—time. There aren't many jobs that give you that kind of freedom."

Of course, not all actors are as talented—or lucky—as Jensen and his dad have been. But for them, things have worked out very well. From the time he was a child, Jensen's striking good looks and outgoing personality have given him a distinct advantage with acting and modeling agents. At age four he began appearing in print and TV ads in the Dallas area. Before long he was doing national commercials as well, for companies like Walmart, Nabisco, and Radio Shack. In high school, he was not only a hot commercial actor, he scored the lead role of Tony in his senior class production of *West Side Story*. (Surprise! Jensen can sing, too!)

But acting was never Jensen's first love. Sports were his true high school passion. He played a lot of football. (When he first left Texas to try acting in Los Angeles, Jensen figured that if things didn't work out, he could always go to college for a degree in sports medicine. Guess those injured athletes are going to have to get well without him!)

"I wasn't one of those people who knew from childhood that I wanted to be an actor. It was just something I did for fun," he says.

Jensen's Texas life took a turn toward the West Coast in the spring of 1995. That's when he attended an acting seminar in Dallas. It was a Friday night, and Jensen wasn't even one of the actors who was invited to the workshop. He just came as the guest of a friend. What happened next was a tale right out of the soaps.

"I spotted a young actor I had invited to attend," Craig Wargo recalls. "He introduced me to a friend whom he had brought along with him—Jensen Ackles. Soon after our introduction, the rest of our staff noticed Jensen as a standout at the seminar."

After the workshop, Craig met Jensen's family, and asked them to let their son move out to Los Angeles after he graduated from high school. It took some convincing, but the Ackleses finally agreed. Jensen hopped a flight to L.A. right after graduation.

But even with a manager who believed in him, Jensen still wasn't sure he wanted to be an actor full time. "I really just came out [to Los Angeles] to please them [the managers at Talent Management Associates]. They were very insistent on me coming out and trying. I figured, 'Oh, I'll just go out and please these guys for a couple of months and move back home.' Little did I know . . ."

Success from the Start

Jensen's very first Los Angeles audition was for a guest-starring part on a syndicated TV show called *Sweet Valley High*. Jensen walked into the audition room an unemployed actor and walked out with the part! If Jensen had headed to L.A. just to test the waters, it was obvious that it was smooth sailing.

Jensen's next audition was for the role of

Malcolm on the NBC series *Mr. Rhodes*. Now what are the chances Jensen would land *both* of his first two Hollywood auditions? Pretty slim. But that's just what happened. Jensen played Malcolm for all of the series' thirteen episodes.

"It [*Mr. Rhodes*] didn't get picked up for a second season, but it was a great gig. Prime time, I mean, whoa!" Jensen exclaims.

Still, after NBC canceled *Mr. Rhodes*, it seemed as though Jensen had emptied his good-luck pot of gold. He went on literally hundreds of auditions between February and May of 1997. All he got was one small role as Cybill Shepherd's godson on an episode of the CBS comedy *Cybill*.

Finally, he found himself in the office of Fran Bascom, who does the casting for *Days of Our Lives*. Jensen remembers that his life-altering audition didn't feel threatening at all.

"I went in and read and it was really nice because Fran didn't get right to the script," he recently recalled in *Soap Opera News*. "We had a conversation, so it made it comfortable for me to read in front of her. Then, when I came back to read for her again, it was like reading with a friend."

Jensen had never gone through anything as lengthy as the audition process for *Days* before. He had to read with several of the actors before he was

☆ Sizzlin' Soap Stars ☆

finally chosen for the coveted role of Eric Brady, Marlena's long-lost son, and twin brother to *Days*'s most conniving female, Sami.

"I loved him instantly," recalls Deidre Hall, who plays Marlena. "He's clever, funny, slightly outrageous, yet respectful. He's sweet, confident, and boyish. The crew loved him before we rolled tape on his first scene. We knew this guy was solid."

If Deidre ever gets tired of being one of the most talented actresses in daytime, she should consider becoming a casting director. Her intuition about Jensen was right on. In fact, soon after Jensen's June 1997 debut on *Days*, *TV Guide* called him "the talent discovery of the summer."

The fans caught on quickly, too—especially one little girl from Texas. Maybe you've heard of her—her name's LeAnn Rimes. Ever since Jensen started on *Days*, the country singer has been singing his praises. She even went so far as to tell *Entertainment Tonight* that she has a crush on Jensen. Later, LeAnn fulfilled one of her big dreams by appearing in a few scenes with Jensen on *Days*. And as if that weren't enough, LeAnn asked Jensen to accompany her to the American Music Awards, which he did. Of course, both stars insist they are just buddies.

Jensen soon started winning awards. After

appearing on *Days of Our Lives* for just four months, Jensen was nominated for an award as Outstanding Male Newcomer by *Soap Opera Digest*. Thanks to fan support, he won the honor at the magazine's annual February awards show. In 1998, he was nominated for a daytime Emmy in the Outstanding Younger Actor category. To be nominated for his first few months on the series was quite an honor. Jensen wasn't too disappointed when he lost out to Jonathan Jackson (*General Hospital*'s Lucky) for the top honors. After all, he knows he has lots of years to try again.

The sudden attention was flattering, but also overwhelming. Jensen found himself the object of female-fan attention like he never imagined. Whole chat rooms were dedicated to his new shorter haircut. Girls were stopping him on the street and acting like they knew him. Jensen was shocked, but he treated the fans with the respect only a true southern gentleman could.

"It's kind of odd," he says of his fan encounters. "Somebody came up to me recently when I was shopping and asked for an autograph. It's kind of like an out-of-body experience. Like, is this really happening to me?"

Jensen has discovered that even when he is out in public, the fans expect him to be at least a little

☆ Sizzlin' Soap Stars ☆

like Eric. So, while he doesn't always dress like his TV counterpart, Jensen does borrow some of Eric's clothing for his own wardrobe, which saves him a bit in the budget department.

Not that Jensen has to worry about cash much these days. His *Days of Our Lives* checks are definitely rolling in. But don't expect this Texan to go Hollywood and start buying mansions. So far, all he's bought himself is a new couch.

"I had this three-hundred-dollar garage-sale piece of junk that smelled rank, had stains, and was a total bachelor couch," he says. "I was like, 'You know what? I'm going to get a nice couch.' So I went out and bought a set. That was my big purchase."

New fans, new clothes, new couches—his first year on *Days* was definitely a banner one for Jensen Ackles. But it wasn't so great for Eric Brady. After all, the only two available females in his age range were his sisters, Carrie and Sami.

Enter Arianne . . . and Katherine

Once the producers of *Days* realized that the show's fans saw Jensen as a major romantic hunk, they decided to give Eric Brady a sexy leading lady with secrets all her own. Her name is Nicole.

The role of Nicole was scripted to be a waitress who had dreams of a modeling career, which meant that the actress playing Nicole had to look like a model. Arianne Zucker fit that bill perfectly. The young actress had been modeling for seven years, since she was sixteen years old.

Like Jensen, Arianne had to go through several auditions before she finally landed the role of Nicole. She started by reading the script for the producers. Then she got called back for a screen test with Jensen. The producers needed Jensen to test with Arianne to see if their chemistry would work on screen.

Because Arianne was a very busy model at the time she auditioned for the role of Nicole, she hadn't seen *Days of Our Lives* in a while. TV just didn't fit into her schedule. So the first time she saw Jensen act was when he came to be part of her screen test. But she took to him immediately. "Jensen is a great actor," Arianne declares. "I am so fortunate to be with an all-around great guy. From the beginning I felt so comfortable with him."

Arianne had plenty of time during that screen test to get to know her future costar. "The screen test took five hours!" she recalls. "We did ten pages together. It had crying, laughing, kissing, and anguished emotion in one scene."

Like Jensen, Arianne was a natural actor. Even though this was her first audition, she got the part. Finally, Eric Brady had a love interest.

Of course, on *Days of Our Lives*, nothing is forever, and these days, Eric and Nicole find themselves fighting to stay together. There's someone new with her eye on Eric. Her name's Taylor, and she usually gets what she wants.

Taylor is played by another former model, Katherine Ellis. She may not look familiar to Eric, but she might to you. Katherine has appeared in videos for Smashing Pumpkins and Rod Stewart. If anyone can break up the lovebirds, she can!

Stay tuned . . .

Jensen's Dreams

So, does this sexy Texan plan on making L.A. his permanent home? Don't bet on it. But don't bet on a quick return to the Lone Star State, either. Jensen's planning on a future in Colorado.

When he's asked where he sees himself in ten years, Jensen is likely to reply, "I'd love to be married and have a kid or two or three. I'd like to move away from Los Angeles—closer to my family—but still be active as far as movies go. I'd definitely like to be in movies."

But ten years is a long time. And a lot can happen between now and then. So, for now, Jensen is just taking things day by day. After all, these days, *Days of Our Lives* is giving Jensen the time of his life!

☆ Sizzlin' Soap Stars ☆

☆ Jensen Ackles ☆
Fast Facts

Birthday: March 1
Hair: Dirty blond
Eyes: Hazel
Height: 6'
Favorite Actor: Harrison Ford
Favorite Actress: Meg Ryan
Favorite Singer: Garth Brooks
Favorite TV Shows: *Friends, Party of Five*
Pet: A rottweiler puppy named Dallas
Favorite Sport: Football (His favorite team is the Dallas Cowboys, natch!)
Favorite Food: Pasta

2

Steve Burton

(Jason Morgan [Quartermaine], *General Hospital*)

General Hospital's Jason Morgan has been involved in some major danger! He was in a car crash that left him without a memory. He practically drowned in a plane crash. He almost died when his car was blown up by competing mobsters, and he's taken on the entire Quartermaine family in a custody battle for Carly's son Michael.

But Jason Morgan has *nothing* on Steve Burton, the man who plays him. Steve is a rugged sportsman, and as such, he's taken his fair share of knocks, too. For instance, there was that time he was playing golf with his *GH* costar Tyler Christopher (Nikolas). Tyler whacked Steve in the nose with a golf club and broke his nose!

"He kind of walked into my backswing," says Tyler, defending himself.

Whatever. The point is, Steve wound up with a broken nose from the ordeal. Luckily, the character Jason was already banged up from a story line on the show, so the broken nose fit right in. And Steve held no grudges—he and Tyler are still golfing buddies.

Besides, surfing fanatic Steve hurts himself plenty, without *anyone's* help. One fall recently caused Steve some major cuts on his oh-so-perfect face. "I took off on a wave, ate it, and got sucked under while the board stayed on top, attached to me on a leash," he explains. "When it came up, the white water caused the board to snap back at me. The point of the surfboard went through my mouth."

Ouch!

As if all that weren't bad enough, the *General Hospital* producers have taken the actor on some locations which proved potentially hazardous to his health. It all started during a location shooting in Los Angeles's Griffith Park. The park was subbing for the East Coast's Adirondack Mountains—where the Quartermaines' private jet had crashed, with Jason and Brenda Barrett inside.

The shoot didn't take very long, but for some members of the crew, it seemed itchingly endless. That's because the location scouts had chosen an area famous for its poison oak!

"There was poison oak everywhere," Steve recalls. "In my mind, I thought I had it for sure because I was itching all day long. A few people got it, but thank God, I didn't. I actually couldn't believe they shot a location there. I guess if Vanessa [Marcil, who played Brenda] or I had gotten it, they could have written it in. Put a big patch on my face or something."

Well, thank goodness they didn't have to do that. Who would want to cover up those cheekbones?!

Steve on the Move

Steve Burton was born in Indianapolis, Indiana. He didn't stay there long. His parents divorced when he was young, and Steve lived with his mother, an optician. According to Steve, "My mother's work involved a lot of transfers."

He's not kidding. By the time he reached his junior year in high school, Steve had attended five schools! (Three in Chicago and two in Cleveland.) Interestingly enough, having such a mobile childhood prepared Steve for an actor's life. While people with office professions often stay in the same place for their whole lives, actors work with new people on every job. Actors need to be flexible and know how to quickly become comfortable in new situations.

But at the time, Steve decided he wanted a more settled lifestyle. And at the age of sixteen he found it in—believe it or not—*Beverly Hills!* Steve moved in with his dad, a disc jockey and real

☆ Sizzlin' Soap Stars ☆

estate manager, and attended famous Beverly Hills High School—a place that Steve admits isn't all that different from its *Beverly Hills 90210* TV counterpart.

"I didn't grow up with money, so I was a bit surprised to see sixteen-year-olds driving Mercedes, Porsches, and BMWs," he admits. "There were car trends. One year everybody would be driving Jeeps. The next year they were all getting around in BMW convertibles."

But Beverly Hills High School taught Steve a lot. And not all of it was academic. He had his first serious girlfriend there. While he won't reveal her name, he does recall working hard to romance her. "When I was a senior in high school, I cut my last three periods of school, went and got 101 roses, and placed them everywhere in my girlfriend's house—I broke into her room because I knew how. I put the roses in her room, in her dresser, and—thornless, of course—under her pillow. Everywhere she would look during the day."

Sounds like something a soap opera character would do, doesn't it?

Even though he had a girlfriend, and a few good buds, Steve recalls feeling out of place at Beverly Hills High School until, on the advice of his dad, he took up acting. Back then acting was just a hobby. That hobby soon became a passion, and

Steve became a member of Beverly Hills High's famous Theatre 40 group.

Ironically, Steve's first acting coach was Brooke Bundy, who once played Diana Taylor on GH. Brooke must have been a good teacher, because before long Steve got some commercial work, which was followed by a regular role on the syndicated situation comedy *Out of This World*. Steve played a blond, sexy, surfer dude for the show's 1987–1990 run. (Did anyone say "type casting"?)

Soon after *Out of This World* was canceled, Steve started acting on the soaps—but not on *General Hospital*. He took on the recurring role of Harris Michaels on *Days of Our Lives*.

Life with the Qs

Steve left *Days of Our Lives* to join the *General Hospital* folks in Port Charles in 1993. He was hired to play Jason Quartermaine, the illegitimate child of Alan Quartermaine and his mistress, Susan Moore.

The character of Jason was born in 1981. Young Jason lived with his mother for a while, but after Susan was murdered in 1983, Alan's wife, Monica Quartermaine, agreed to raise the baby with Alan as their own son.

Of course, that would have made Jason only ten years old when twenty-one-year-old Steve auditioned for the role. But soaps have a way of quickly aging children so that their story lines are more exciting.

"*General Hospital* decided to speed up the aging process, so they just brought me back from boarding school older," Steve explains.

Actually, Steve originally auditioned for the role of A. J. Quartermaine, Alan and Monica's eldest son. "I was fairly close to getting that part," he remembers. "Then they decided to bring back Jason."

Years later Steve met actress Gail Ramsey (she used the name Gail Rae Carlson back in the 1980s), who played Susan Moore. "It was so weird," Steve says. "I had heard all about her: how Alan had had an affair, how [Jason] had come about, how she got shot in the head. It was like a link. I got chills. We had a nice talk."

When Steve first took on the role of Jason Quartermaine, Jason was the nice brother. The clean brother. The brother who was going to med school and was going to be the only true do-gooder in the megadysfunctional Quartermaine family.

And then came the car crash!

Jason ~~Quartermaine~~ Morgan

From an actor's point of view, the character of Jason was not very challenging. He was a nice guy—period. But even with so little to do, Steve's acting ability showed through. As Stuart Damon, who plays Jason's father, Alan, told *Daytime TV* magazine, "Steve Burton had been on the show two months, but all the attention was going to Gerald Hopkins, and later Sean Kanan, as A. J. I went to the producers and to the heads of ABC in New York. I told them, 'Steve is the star. You are missing the boat. This kid is not only an incredible actor, but he has the discipline, and will blow you off the map if you let him.'"

Stuart's pleading must have had some effect on the producers, because in early 1996, Jason was in a serious accident when the car driven by his drunken brother A. J. slammed into a tree. The accident caused permanent amnesia. Jason Quartermaine no longer felt any attachment to the people who claimed to be his family. He changed his name to Jason Morgan and began working for mob boss Sonny Corinthos. Eventually he took over the mob and found love with Robin Scorpio.

It's no wonder Steve says that Jason's car crash was "the best thing that ever happened to me." Not only was Steve able to stretch as an actor, but his acting was finally recognized by his peers. In 1997 he received his first daytime Emmy nomination as Outstanding Young Actor in a Drama Series. Steve didn't win that time around, but in

1998, he was nominated again—this time as Best Supporting Actor. (At the age of twenty-seven, Steve no longer qualified as a "young" actor, although his character is still quite young.)

The new category proved the charm Steve needed. He won the Emmy—much to his own surprise.

"It was like my entire body was numb," he says of winning. "My head just kind of fell into my hands with disbelief. I thought for sure I wasn't going to win. I remember giving hugs to Vanessa and Ingo [Marcil and Rademacher, GH's Brenda and Jax, the presenters], but it all happens so fast. I just tried to thank everyone I could think of, so many people have been supportive."

One person Steve was sure to thank was his fiancée, Sheree Guston, whom he met while she was working as an intern at ABC. After the Emmy Awards the happy couple (who plan to wed this year) headed down to Mexico for some much needed R&R. Steve brought his Emmy statue along—maybe so he could convince himself that it wasn't all just a dream.

"It's funny, but the morning after the Emmys, when I woke up I had fallen asleep holding it and it was still there on my pillow. I kept it with us in out hotel room throughout the trip."

After the trip, Steve put the Emmy over his fireplace. He says, "I look at it all the time."

If TV critics are to be believed, Steve had better make more room on that shelf. According to *TV Guide*, Steve follows in the tradition of some of our greatest actors. The magazine reported that "Burton plays baby mafioso Jason Morgan on *General Hospital* with the steely nerve of [James] Cagney, the world weariness of [Humphrey] Bogart, and the sulky, sexy danger of [Robert] Mitchum."

Making Movies

Over the years, Steve has managed to take some time off from his *GH* gig to do two feature films—*CyberTracker* (1994) and *CyberTracker 2* (1995). These science fiction films allowed Steve a chance to try some martial arts and action.

"I've been playing Jason long enough to satisfy my dramatic side, so it's a lot of fun to add some action to my acting platter," he admits.

There was some danger involved in making the films. And you know how Steve loves danger! "[Director and producer] Rick Pepin is terrific. He trusted me to do my own stunts. I'm learning that hitting the ground during rehearsal on a mattress hurts a lot less than doing it just a few minutes later and landing on a cement floor," Steve admits, adding, "It hurts a lot more, but it's also a lot more fun."

Steve's done some modeling, too. He's posed for Steve Burton calendars since 1996, appeared in *Playgirl* (relax—he was covered up in the photo spread), and was featured with former castmate Sean Kanan (ex–A. J.) in the coffee table book *Perfect Face*.

Steve won't lie about it—he truly enjoyed his movie and modeling breaks, particularly the chance to play a character so unlike Jason. But don't worry about Steve leaving the *GH* set in the near future. As he told *TV Guide*, "Sure I'm looking for other opportunities. But this role has turned out so great, it's spoiled me."

It's spoiled Steve's fans, too. After all, Jason is exciting, sincere, and caring. Best of all, he looks like the dashing Steve Burton.

☆ Steve Burton ☆
Fast Facts

Birthday: June 28
Height: 5'11"
Eyes: Dark blue
Favorite Foods: Swordfish, steak, chicken (He has been known to use the prop ovens on the set to make his special barbecue chicken.)
Favorite Sport: Surfing
Idea of a Perfect Weekend: Spending time at his uncle's cabin in Big Bear, going skiing or snow boarding, and then relaxing by the fire

Tyler Christopher
(Nikolas Cassidine, *General Hospital*)

Ask Tyler Christopher's fiancée, Vanessa Marcil (ex-Brenda, *General Hospital*), what she finds most sexy about her handsome husband-to-be and you might be surprised at her answer. She won't say it's his brooding brown eyes or perfectly toned muscles.

"I think the most beautiful thing about Tyler is his simplicity and his complete lack of awareness of how brilliantly talented he is," she told *Soap Opera* magazine recently.

Simplicity? That's not exactly a Hollywood buzzword, is it? But the truth is, Tyler Christopher is not your typical Hollywood star. Tyler is a small-town boy from Delaware, Ohio, and as far as he's concerned, that's the way he wants to be perceived.

"I have an old-fashioned way of treating people," he explains. "It comes from the fact that I grew up in a small town. I think what people find beautiful about me is my kindness towards them and my unselfish attitude."

Maybe. But those eyes and pecs don't hurt!

The Small-Town Boy

Tyler Christopher was born in Joliet, Illinois, but he was raised in Delaware, Ohio, not far from the city of Columbus. Tyler describes his hometown as being "a very small, Midwestern, conservative kind of country little town. It's one of those places if you blink, you'll miss it."

Sounds like the kind of place where people raise corn, not soap opera stars, right? As a matter of fact, Tyler says that when he was growing up, acting "never crossed my mind. Not one bit." He wanted to be a baseball player.

Tyler's childhood was textbook normal. Unlike the only-child character of Nikolas Cassidine, whom he plays every day on *General Hospital*, Tyler grew up with lots of sibs. He's the youngest of four, and he freely admits he was the troublemaker of the bunch. Luckily, his brother and his two sisters made sure he didn't get into too much trouble. To this day, Tyler says his older brother is his hero.

Tyler's parents put great stock in education. His mom works at Ohio Wesleyan University. His dad is an engineer. His brothers and sisters all went on

☆ Sizzlin' Soap Stars ☆

to college and became teachers. So you can imagine his parents' surprise (and dismay!) when Tyler packed his bags and left for Hollywood after only two years as an economics major at Ohio Wesleyan University.

"It wasn't that I was doing badly," Tyler explains. "I was a good student. But you just know when something's not right for you. I had a cousin who knew that he wanted to be an actor all his life. He moved to Los Angeles right out of high school. He said to me, 'Maybe you should give acting a try.' Seeing that he was having some moderate success, I thought maybe I could make it, too."

But that Hollywood brass ring is pretty tough to grab on to. After just two months, Tyler packed his bags again and headed for home.

"I really didn't give it a chance," he says now.

Tyler didn't go back to school. He spent his time bartending in Columbus, and working construction. He also ran up a pretty hefty credit card bill. "I really hurt myself in the past getting into debt," Tyler acknowledges. "I went in my mailbox . . . and there was a preapproved credit card with my name on it. It looked like gold to me. It was crazy, when you think about it. I mean, how could I get one? I didn't even have a job. It didn't dawn on me that they give everyone one."

Charge! Soon Tyler was buying things all over

town. "It buried me," he admits. Tyler charged so much he spent many of his first year's GH paychecks paying back creditors.

Los Angeles: Take 2

It didn't take Tyler long to realize that he had made a big mistake leaving Los Angeles. "I was so miserable, unclear and unfocused about my life," he recalls. "I had no skills and no direction. People thought that I was lazy, but that wasn't it. I was searching for my dream."

That dream finally led him back to L.A. And this time, Tyler was determined to stick it out. The first eighteen months he was in California, Tyler didn't have much work, but he did land a small role in an independent film called *Common Bonds*. He played "a rebel teenager who always got everyone else in trouble but never got in trouble himself," Tyler explains. After the film, he spent time doing industrial shows for companies like Pepsi.

Finally he got a call from his agent about an audition at *General Hospital*. At the time, Tyler had no idea who Nikolas Cassidine was. But he knew that GH was the big time. So he hired an acting coach to help him get ready for the audition, and he hit up friends for information on the Cassidines.

"I never watched the soaps," he explains. "Basically everything I knew about them was from what other people were telling me. I have a friend back home who is a big fan of *General Hospital*. When I told her I was first going out for this audition, she was trying to decipher where I would fit in. She did a good job. She probably knows more about the people I work with every day than I do."

Tyler's first *GH* audition was in April 1996. He remembers the audition process as being long and nerve-wracking. "I auditioned in April with Mark Teschner, who is head of casting, and didn't hear anything for quite a while. They were trying all different kinds of ways [to go with Nikolas], different age groups, different looks. It wasn't until the middle of June that I went back and read again for [Executive Producer] Wendy Riche and for the rest of the producers. Then I went back one more time and did a different scene, one that was a bit more difficult. And then, like not even a week later, I screen-tested with about four or five other people. Two days later, I got the part."

Nikolas Cassidine is a teenager. Tyler is in his twenties. But he believes that being slightly older than Nikolas puts him at an advantage as an actor.

"I just try to pull from experiences from my past and incorporate them into Nikolas," he explains. "I try to make it real and add a sense of reality to the character from my own experience. Younger people react to certain situations in a different way and I have to remind myself of that. Teenagers, including myself when I was one, react a lot more defensively in a lot of situations, and I have to remind myself to keep doing that."

Nikolas Saves the Day

Nikolas Cassidine's arrival at *General Hospital* was due to an emergency. Laura Spencer's daughter, Lesley Lu, had a life-threatening illness. She needed a blood transfusion from a relative. None of her family had a matching blood type—except for a long-lost son Laura had given birth to when she was involved with the Cassidines. Nikolas left Greece, flew to Port Charles, and literally saved his half sister's life.

It was a gallant entrance. Unfortunately the actor playing Nikolas did not have a quite as wonderful first day on the job.

"The hardest day for me was the first day of taping," Tyler admitted to *Soap Opera Weekly*. "I was with the babies who play Lesley Lu. I don't have any little sisters, and I haven't been around little kids much. The director told me to just talk to her and make her smile. On the final take she had her finger up her nose the whole time I was talking to her. I was smiling—actually laughing—at her, but trying to hold it back."

☆ Sizzlin' Soap Stars ☆

And that wasn't the only trial he faced on that first day. Just getting out of the elevator was difficult. After saying his lines on the hospital set, Tyler was instructed to exit the scene by walking onto the elevator. He did, and the doors shut behind him. When the director shouted "cut," Tyler waited for the elevator doors to open again and let him out. And he kept on waiting. "I didn't realize there was a secret door in the back," he laughs. "I figured since they'd put me in there, they'd let me out. Everyone got a good laugh out of that one."

Tyler obviously learned quickly that when it comes to soaps, nothing is as it seems.

Romance!

Okay, so at first everything didn't go smoothly for Tyler. But those early days on *General Hospital* did bring someone special into his life—Vanessa Marcil. Back in 1996, Vanessa played Brenda on the soap. Brenda was torn between two lovers—Sonny, a mob boss, and Jax, a wealthy businessman. But in real life Vanessa was totally single. And not particularly looking.

Vanessa was the first cast member to try to make Tyler feel at home. "I always try to be friendly to the new people. I think about how scary it is to be new, while the rest of us are like a family, hanging out and talking all the time. So I said, 'Welcome to the show,' and he had that kind of scared look on his face," she recalls, adding that from the time she met Tyler, she knew he was someone special. "Some people you meet and you automatically know you are going to be friends with them."

Friends? Just *friends*?

Actually that's exactly how Tyler and Vanessa started out. "Romance blossomed from our friendship, which is something I don't think either of us had ever experienced before," Vanessa explains.

Before long, Vanessa was sporting a diamond engagement ring, which Tyler had designed himself. And while they haven't married yet—their busy schedules keep breaking into the wedding plans—the two have agreed on the kind of wedding they want to have.

Tyler feels that besides the cost, putting on such a big wedding "takes away from the true meaning of the whole thing. So we're just going to have the people closest to us and have a very quaint, beautiful wedding."

New Challenges

Vanessa stayed with *General Hospital* until the fall of 1998, when she left to take a part on *Beverly*

Hills 90210. And although she was ready to leave, both she and Tyler regret that their characters never shared a story line. In fact, they had only one big scene together. Brenda and Nikolas, who were both raised without mothers, bumped into one another and started to talk about their shared experience. Tyler and Vanessa have as good of an on-screen chemistry as they do off screen. They nailed the scene in just one take.

While Vanessa's leaving *GH* was tough for Tyler, he's content to stay right where he is. Tyler sees *GH* as a true learning experience. After all, he's already gotten the chance to act opposite some of the most talented people in the business.

"I've gotten to work with Stephen Nichols, Tony Geary, and Genie Francis [Stefan, Luke, and Laura]. At first I was like—*whoa!* But they were so warm that they made me feel comfortable. They're all so calm and confident in what they are doing. They know they're good. They don't need to say it. You can see it in their work. I want to get to that point. I've learned more from watching and working with them than I have in my whole life—in any aspect," he declares.

And Tyler is putting those lessons to good use. Since he took on the role of Nikolas, Tyler has performed in the Los Angeles stage production of *Loot*, a British dark comedy. He also landed a role in the independent film *Catfish in Black Bean Sauce*. *Catfish* was shot in just twenty-three days, and Tyler didn't miss any work on GH. It was hard for Tyler to move back and forth between his role on GH and his part in *Catfish*, because the two characters were so different.

"[In *Catfish*] I play the roommate of this guy who comes home from all his trials and tribulations of the day, and we have these nice, funny scenes to lighten things up. I'm not involved in the premise of the film, but I do get to do a lot of interesting stuff throughout. I think it will surprise a lot of people because it's so different from what they're used to seeing me do as Nikolas," he explains.

His next movie job was in a short film called *The Gift*, which premiered at the Sundance Film Festival. Tyler played a blind sculptor who is afraid that if he regains his sight, he'll lose his talent. The film was cowritten, directed, and produced by *Days of Our Lives* actress Tanya Boyd. Tanya knows all about soap opera schedules, so she made sure to work around Tyler's days on the GH set.

Tyler's character in *The Gift* may have been afraid of the downside of change, but having a starring role in *General Hospital* has definitely changed Tyler for the better. He feels he's a stronger actor than ever, and he truly loves his craft. He's got a beautiful fiancée, and he's made new friends, like GH's Steve Burton (Jason), with whom he plays a lot of golf.

Tyler's also got a new name. Fans who regularly check out the GH cast list will recall that when Nikolas Cassidine first arrived, he was played by Tyler Baker. Tyler Baker *is* Tyler Christopher. Christopher is Tyler's middle name. There have been all sorts of rumors about the reason Tyler changed his name, but he has never publicly said why. He just claims it as a personal thing. And not really a big deal, either.

"I wanted to [change my name] for a long time, and I don't really have a specific reason why," he says. "I started to do it a few years back. You have to go through a big process through the courts. I started [the legal process] before the show, and it happened after I was on the show."

So what does the future hold for Tyler? Well, first and foremost, there's his marriage to Vanessa. The two both say that they want kids someday, but not for a while. For now, they are busy decorating their new homestead, an old house from the 1920s with thick walls and very few windows.

"It probably sounds depressing, but I hate light—light bulbs, sunlight," he says. "If I had my way the whole world would be lit with candles."

On the work front, Tyler continues to strive at

becoming a better actor. He studies constantly with an acting coach and is looking into doing more movies.

"Success increased my self-confidence and opened me emotionally," he told *Soap Opera Digest*. "Then I fell in love with acting. Now that I know this is my passion, my love, my career—I want to go for it. This is the only thing I want to do."

☆ Sizzlin' Soap Stars ☆

☆ Tyler Christopher ☆
Fast Facts

Birthday: November 11

High School Yearbook: Voted both "most likely never to be married" *and* "most likely to be married more than once." (What's *that* about?)

Hobbies: Football, golf, and writing

Favorite Food: Anything with garlic

What He Would Like to Change About Himself: His impatience

Favorite Actor: Marlon Brando

Favorite Season: Summer

Greatest Wish: To become the best at whatever he does

Favorite Movie: *Braveheart*

Nickname: Chief (given to him by his big brother, because their family is part Native American)

4

Adrienne Frantz

(Ambrosia "Amber" Moore,
The Bold and the Beautiful)

Does Adrienne Frantz ever sleep? All you have to do is look at her resume to see that this girl is one big ball of talented energy. She's a TV star, a movie actress, a singer, a writer, a former beauty queen, a professional clown . . .

Yep, you read right—a clown! When she was a teenager, Adrienne performed in a clown costume at kids' parties. Even now, if you asked her, she could probably whip up a balloon animal or two for you!

But the truth is, with her busy lifestyle, Adrienne doesn't really have time for clowning around anymore. If you live outside the Los Angeles area, you probably know Adrienne as Amber on *The Bold and the Beautiful*. But you might not know that she's also the lead singer in her own Los Angeles band. And although Adrienne is still best known as Amber, her popularity as a singer is growing.

☆ Sizzlin' Soap Stars ☆

Recently, a panel of music industry heavyweights voted Adrienne L.A.'s best unsigned female vocalist. Adrienne's been working hard to live up to the title. She and her band have recorded an independent album, and lately Adrienne's been spending her evenings playing sold-out gigs at L.A.'s famous Whiskey Club and in Hawaii. As if that weren't enough, keep your ears ready for the soundtrack to Meg Ryan's new film, *Angel's Freeway*. Adrienne will have the lead song!

Adrienne admits that being a soap opera siren hasn't exactly hurt her music career. "I admit that I am fortunate to be a popular daytime television star. But in the end, it is the music and my band's incredible talent level that will carry us to the big time. That is what the music industry looks for," she insists.

If that's so, Adrienne is going straight to the top of the charts. Of course, she's been climbing that success ladder for a long, long time.

Growing up with Music

Adrienne has been singing since she was just two years old. "My mom was listening to 'Light My Fire' by the Doors," Adrienne recalls. "I just picked up the melody and started singing it. From that point on, my mom would play Doors albums whenever I asked, and I just started memorizing their songs. To this day I am a huge fan of that band—I still listen to their music just about every day."

Now, lots of kids sing along with their parents' albums, but they don't wind up singing the national anthem in front of thousands of Detroit Pistons fans at age twelve. Of course, most kids don't have Adrienne's drive. By the age of three, this only child was holding private dance recitals for the neighbors. By ten she had become a minicelebrity in Detroit (the city nearest to her Mount Clemens, Michigan, home), starring in local stage productions of *Oklahoma*, *Li'l Abner*, and *Dracula* and participating in beauty pageants. She soon became a regular at Pistons games, belting out "The Star-Spangled Banner" and cheering her home team.

It was then that Adrienne knew she had to be a performer. She was so sure she'd be a success she bet a high school pal one thousand dollars that she would be a huge star. (Have you collected on that one yet, Adrienne? You should!) Eventually, Michigan just became too small a venue for Adrienne's talents. She yearned for the bright lights of New York City. So at age sixteen she moved to the Big Apple and started making commercials. That led to her first big acting job, as Hermia in the New York Youth Theatre's

☆ Sizzlin' Soap Stars ☆

production of *A Midsummer Night's Dream*. Making your New York stage debut in a Shakespearean play could be daunting to some actresses, but not Adrienne. She has always had confidence. As she herself says, "I put my mind to something and then just carry it through."

Still, even with those early successes, Adrienne was afraid to put all her eggs into the show biz basket. So she enrolled in New York's Marymount College. She was all set to start her freshman year when she got a very exciting phone call.

Beach Party!

Adrienne had been asked to audition for a new soap opera—the first daytime show produced by famed TV mogul Aaron Spelling.

Only a complete moron would give up a chance to work with Aaron Spelling. As the producer of shows like *The Mod Squad*, *Charlie's Angels*, *Beverly Hills 90210*, and *Melrose Place*, he'd helped create amazing careers for Peggy Lipton, Farrah Fawcett, Jennie Garth, and Heather Locklear.

Adrienne walked out of Marymount College, and never looked back.

Aaron Spelling's new show was called *Sunset Beach*. Adrienne was quickly cast as Tiffany Thorne, a troubled runaway on the show. She was the love interest of Randy Spelling, Aaron's son, and one of the early breakaway stars of *Sunset Beach*.

Adrienne loved the character of the free-spirited Tiffany. "She's a homeless runaway from an abusive family," Adrienne described the character at the time. "She doesn't trust anybody. And she's always looking for love in the wrong places—going after people for their money and stuff. She's also kind of backstabbing. She's a vixen in training."

Adrienne became an immediate star when *Sunset Beach* launched in 1997. The *Los Angeles Times* did a feature on Adrienne and Randy saying, "Since Aaron Spelling's latest soap opera, *Sunset Beach*, started in January, it is the show's two youngest stars—Randy Spelling and Adrienne Frantz—who have been causing all kinds of trouble in the world of daytime drama."

And hey, trouble is what daytime drama is all about, isn't it?

Adrienne's Bold Move

Adrienne's wandering spirit wasn't satisfied by life at the *Beach*. So, after less than a year on *Sunset Beach*, this beauty boldly left for CBS's hot soap, *The Bold and the Beautiful*.

Adrienne loved just about everything about her

☆ Sizzlin' Soap Stars ☆

The Bold and the Beautiful character—she was a singer and just a little trashy. She was from the wrong side of the tracks and not about to let anything keep her down. In fact, the only thing Adrienne did not like about her new character was her name—Ambrosia.

"I hate marshmallows, for one thing," Adrienne explains. (Ambrosia is a type of snack that is made with marshmallows and fruits.) "Luckily, on the show they usually call me Amber. They only call me Ambrosia if they want to piss [the character] off!"

At first, the character of Amber did not have her own story line. She was intertwined with the story lines of other characters. But once the audience began noticing Adrienne, the fan mail starting piling up. The producers at *The Bold and the Beautiful* knew they had a hot star on their hands. If the audience wanted to see her in a juicy role, the producers were more than glad to give it to them.

The story line that began in the summer of 1998 was, as the show's producer, Bradley Bell, once described it, "a controversial story that I think is a daytime first, involving birth control and teen pregnancy."

The story line was a definite sizzler. Amber found herself pregnant. But who was the father:

Raymond (played by guest-star teen rapper Usher) or Rick (played by Adrienne's *B&B* costar Jacob Young)?

The audience was fascinated by the story. Adrienne was honored that the producers had trusted her with a story line that included drinking, teen pregnancy, and an interracial relationship.

Unfortunately, Adrienne was surprised by some fans' reactions to the story. She told *Soaps in Depth* that she had received some hate mail from fans, because her character had an affair with a black character. Adrienne was saddened by the mail, and her response was pure Adrienne. She simply told the fans to "find something better to do with your time!"

Adrienne was ecstatic when Amber's life became so complicated. "It's great!" she exclaims. "My character actually has her own story line now instead of being intertwined with other people."

As her character became more and more prominent, Adrienne found herself being a reference source for the show's writers. It was up to her to make sure that Amber sounded like a real teenager.

"One day [the script] had me saying some fifties word or something, and I was like, 'Nah, this is what you say,'" she explains, proudly adding, "I think this is probably the most realistic soap opera that's out now."

Making It in the Movies

You might think that between daily 7:00 A.M. calls on the set of *The Bold and the Beautiful* and playing gigs at night, Adrienne might be too wiped out to do anything else. But if that's what you're thinking—you're wrong. Because somewhere in her 24/7 work life, Adrienne has found time to do film work, too.

In 1998, Adrienne took on the role of Sheila in the independent feature *Jimmy Zip*, a movie about a runaway pyromaniac who teams up with a sculptor to take over the art world. Her costars included Alyssa Milano and Brendan Fletcher.

Adrienne also played a small part in *Speedway Junky*, which starred fellow TV teen Jonathan Taylor Thomas (*Home Improvement*). That movie proved dangerous when Adrienne and Jonathan did a scene that called for them to share a pipe of marijuana. Jonathan passed the lit pipe to Adrienne and promptly dropped it in her palm. Adrienne ended up with second-degree burns. It just proves that drugs—even fake movie drugs—are hazardous to your health!

Adrienne would like to do more movie work—

perhaps even behind the camera. Someday she'd like to produce and direct films. She's also been working on a screenplay that she hopes to shop around town.

As for her big-screen *acting* dreams, Adrienne does have one giant fantasy—to do a movie with Val Kilmer. "He's my absolute favorite actor!" she admits.

Well, while she's waiting for Val to call, Adrienne can keep herself busy helping Amber adjust to motherhood, and writing songs for her next album. She's also scheduled to do a number of charity appearances for the March of Dimes. Her agent continues to send her movie scripts to consider, and there's that screenplay she's writing . . .

Hey Adrienne, why not sleep in this Saturday? We think you could use the rest!

☆ Sizzlin' Soap Stars ☆

☆ Adrienne Frantz ☆
Fast Facts

Birthday: June 7
Height: 5'4"
Eyes: Blue/yellow (Adrienne calls them cat's eyes.)
Pets: Two cats: Josie Wales and Cuddles Patricia
Favorite Sports: Skiing and softball
Favorite Band: The Doors
Favorite Cartoon Character: Mickey Mouse
Secret Obsession: Clothes ("I could wear something different every single day of the year," she admits.)
Hobbies: Writing poetry and going to concerts

5

Rebecca Herbst

(Elizabeth Webber, *General Hospital*)

When most kids want a new toy, they write letters to Santa or wait for their birthdays. Not Becky Herbst. When she was six years old, she came up with a much smarter plan. She told her mother she wanted to make commercials. That way she could play with lots of new toys.

Pretty clever, huh? Of course it helped that Becky's older sister, Jennifer, was already an actress—she appeared in the Disney video, *Mousercize*. One of the *Mousercize* producers helped Becky get a role on a commercial. Unfortunately, that first commercial wasn't exactly what Becky had in mind. Instead of playing with a cool new doll, Becky found herself hawking Banner toilet paper!

Still, the young actress's career was launched. For the next thirteen years Becky toiled away, making more than sixty commercials. She appeared in educational videos, the TV movie *Dan-*

☆ Sizzlin' Soap Stars ☆

ielle Steele's Kaleidoscope with Jaclyn Smith, and the feature film *Why Me?*, which starred Christopher Lloyd. She also had guest spots on shows like *LA Law*, *Beverly Hills 90210*, *Step by Step*, and *Boy Meets World*.

Believe it or not, during that time, acting was not Becky's only extracurricular activity. She was also a very successful competitive figure skater. Throughout most of her childhood, Becky rose before dawn to get over to the ice-skating rink and practice her figure eights. Skating, school, acting . . . yikes! It's amazing the girl got any sleep.

It's kind of rare for one person to be talented in so many different ways. And yet everyone who knew Becky back then thought of her as totally normal and not stuck up at all. That was thanks in part to her mother's strict rules. Becky's mom has always been her manager. And as her manager, Mom had the right to pull the plug on Becky's career if her grades (or her attitude) slipped. It's not like Becky was given a private tutor or anything, either. She had to pull her weight at a tough private parochial school.

By the time she reached sixteen, Becky knew she had to make a choice—acting or skating. You see, Becky is born under the star sign of Taurus. And like most Taurians, Becky can be a bit of a perfectionist. She is absolutely miserable when she's forced to do things halfway. Since both acting and skating require total dedication, Becky couldn't do both. Luckily for her fans, Becky felt her heart was in acting.

Becky made the right choice. Just three years later, in 1996, Becky finally found herself with a full-time acting job. But she wasn't playing a teen beauty queen or anything glamorous like that. Becky was playing a space alien!

Space Cases was a Nickelodeon show that was already in its second season when Becky joined the cast. Becky's character, Suzee, was an alien from the planet Yensid. The character was first introduced as the invisible friend of one of the original cast members. But Suzee soon became quite visible. In fact, with her rainbow hair and fishlike gills, she was hard to miss.

"I had purple, blue, and red stripes in my hair that were permanently dyed," Becky recalls. "My hair was like that for four whole months!"

Playing a teen alien on a Nickelodeon sci-fi show may not be every actress's dream role, but it did force Becky to stretch her acting talents. After all, it's not many young actresses who can say things like, "You see these gills? With these gills I can breathe in anything, except for the vacuum of space," and really sound like they mean it!

Space Cases was canceled at the end of its second season. Becky then went on to play the troubled teen Kristin in *Brotherly Love*, a series starring the Lawrence brothers (Joey, Matthew, and Andy). After playing Kristin in only seven episodes, Becky received notice that *Brotherly Love* had been canceled. It was a major blow, since Becky had hoped that being part of a show that featured such famous teen idols would be a big break for her. Still, playing Kristin had shown TV casting agents that perky Becky could also play tough and troubled characters—something that was to come in very handy for her next big role.

Welcome to Port Charles

In 1998, two new sisters joined the residents of the fictional city of Port Charles on *General Hospital*. One was sweet, sensitive Sarah Webber, played by Jennifer Sky. The other was scheming, dangerous Elizabeth "Lizzy" Webber, a force to be reckoned with. The role of Lizzy went to Becky.

From the first day on the set, Becky poured her heart into the character of Lizzy. She made viewers see that there was more to the character than just the venom and scheming the script portrayed. Lizzy was jealous because everyone was naturally drawn to Sarah. Everyone, that is, except *General Hospital*'s viewers. Even though the early story lines featured Sarah far more than Lizzy, audiences soon became intrigued with the darker, angrier sister. Before long, Sarah was shipped off to Europe to visit her parents and Lizzy was left in Port Charles on her own.

The *General Hospital* writers noted the popularity of Lizzy's character and decided to run with it. They approached Becky with a story line idea that would really stretch the young star's acting chops to the limit, forcing her to reveal feelings she had never explored before.

The Rape of Lizzy Webber

The writers had planned an intense story line for the summer of 1998. Lizzy Webber was going to be raped. Becky would be responsible for showing all of the emotions a young, frightened rape victim goes through.

Filming the aftermath of the rape was one of the hardest things Becky ever had to do. The horror of the event was clear in everything that appeared on the set that day.

"All I had to do was look at my body," Becky explains. "The makeup was incredible. The bruises were amazing. My nylons were ripped and the [fake] blood was dripping down my leg. All I had to do was look down, and I was there. When my mom saw me, she began to cry."

Luckily, Becky did not have to work through the scenes alone. She had the help of her costar,

☆ Sizzlin' Soap Stars ☆

Jonathan Jackson, who plays Lucky Spencer on *GH*. Jonathan is five years younger than Becky. And although he was only sixteen at the time the rape scenes were filmed, Becky depended on him to help pull her through.

"I forget about Jonathan's age completely when I'm working with him," she insists. "Jonathan and I have really bonded through this whole thing. I really depended on him to help me through it. I think he knew I was scared to death to act this out, and he was right there with me, just as leery, but still trying to be the male role model. When I get on the set every morning, as soon as I'm Liz, I just want to be hugged by him."

Playing a character who is involved with a member of *GH*'s illustrious Spencer clan has also given Becky a chance to work with a true soap opera legend—Anthony Geary. He's best known as Luke Spencer. That's as in *Luke and Laura*. And let's face it. When it comes to soap opera romances, none is more famous than that of Luke and Laura Spencer. So, working with Tony Geary was more than just a little intimidating for Becky.

"[The scene in which Lizzy talks to Luke after she has been raped] was really only the second time I'd worked with Tony," Becky explains. "Doing something I'd never done before in front of

[him] was nerve-wracking. I mean he's *Luke*, y'know? When I was growing up, I never watched soaps, but I still knew who Luke and Laura were. So this is just so weird for me. I really admire him. He's a great actor."

After filming the scenes that related to Lizzy's rape, Becky was emotionally drained. "After I taped those first rape scenes I went home and slept for fourteen hours. Part of me wasn't sure that I could pull this off because I've never done anything like this. But I feel so honored that *General Hospital* trusted me with this story."

The weeks that followed didn't get any easier for Lizzy—or Becky. The writers sent Lizzy on a search for the identity of her rapist.

It took months for GH to reveal it. But even after he was jailed, on unrelated charges, Lizzy continued to be affected by the rape—as any real-life victim would be. That means Becky will be able to stretch herself even further as an actress. And because Liz and Lucky's relationship is becoming more and more intense, Becky will continue to have the opportunity to work with amazing actors like Jonathan, Tony, and Genie Francis (who plays Lucky's mom, Laura Spencer). As Becky explains it, "Once you're in with the Spencer family, you're going to be in for life."

Of course, the fictional Spencers aren't the only family Becky has joined since becoming part of the GH cast. She's also gotten pretty tight with her cast members. She and Jonathan pal around quite often—they went to *The Mask of Zorro* premiere together, and she has designated herself his personal shopper. Becky took Jonathan shopping for the 1998 GH fan-club party, choosing khaki slacks and a black ribbed T-shirt. "I told him he couldn't wear tennis shoes with it, but he did anyway," she laughs.

But let's face it, even though Lucky and Liz seem perfectly matched, Jonathan *is* five years younger than Becky. So real-life romance is unlikely. Becky did have a fling with fellow GHer Ingo Rademacher (Jax) for a while, however. They were quite an item, even showing up at the *Soap Opera Digest* Awards together. (Becky wore a gown she designed herself. Is this girl talented or what?!)

These days, Becky's going it solo. "Ingo and I are no longer technically dating, but he's more a part of my life than before," Becky explains. "We just figured out that we're a lot better friends this way, and our friendship means the world to me. This change in our relationship was totally mutual and we both view it as a positive thing. We still hang out—but as friends."

☆ Nancy Krulik ☆

Things You Never Knew

Becky's fans might think they know her—after all, she wears so much of her emotion on her sleeve when playing Lizzy Webber. But the truth is, Becky has some secrets. Like the fact that she's really timid. "I am extremely shy," Becky admits. "And I have a severe case of stage fright."

She's also a real worrier. Recently she told *Soap Opera Digest* that when it comes to stress, "I worry everything about nothing."

Becky is an avid animal lover. She has four cats, two dogs, a rabbit, and a squirrel named Beaker, whom she rescued when she found the animal injured with a dislocated hip and broken leg.

As for Lizzy Webber's totally modern look, that's one place she and Becky definitely part company. Becky is more the romantic sort. In fact, she insists that "I was not meant to live in this era. [If I could live in any era] it would be the early 1900s. The clothing was fascinating. It had style and class, and it looked great on any figure." Becky says she likes men from that bygone era as well. Her taste runs toward "a manly man who would decorate and design a house with me."

And just in case you were wondering, Becky

☆ Sizzlin' Soap Stars ☆

does still visit the ice-skating rink once in a while. But if you want to catch her skating routines, you're better off looking around the beachside boardwalks near L.A. Becky does most of her skating on Rollerblades these days. She saves the icy stuff for the stares Lizzy Webber gives to anyone who threatens her and Lucky!

☆ Rebecca Herbst ☆
Fast Facts

Birthday: May 12
Height: 5'2"
Eye Color: Blue
Hair Color: Light brown
Favorite Snack: Cheese and crackers
Favorite TV Show: *Bewitched*
What She Considers Her Best Trait: Her compassion for people and animals
What She Considers Her Worst Trait: Being grumpy in the morning
Least Favorite Thing to Do: Vacuum
Hobby: Rollerblading

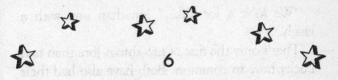

6
Jonathan Jackson
(Lucky Spencer, *General Hospital*)

Jonathan Jackson wants his fans to know that he and Lucky Spencer are not one and the same.

"Lucky is a lot more black and white in his personality than I am. I try to have more gray areas. He either likes or hates something," Jonathan claims.

And these days, Lucky is filled with hate. He found out his father raped his mother before they were married. Now Lucky feels betrayed by his parents, GH's Luke and Laura. He's so angry he can barely speak to them.

But *Jonathan* has a really tight relationship with *his* folks.

"My parents have an incredible marriage," Jonathan says of his parents, Jeanine and Ricky Lee Jackson. "Our family is very, very close."

So, do Jonathan and Lucky have anything in common?

"We look a lot alike," Jonathan says with a laugh.

That's only the first of *two* things Jonathan and Lucky have in common. Both have also had their own bouts of sibling rivalry with their older brothers.

In Lucky's case, he was a teenager before he even *knew* he had an older brother. Nikolas Cassidine was Laura's son from a previous relationship with Stefan Cassidine (who Nikolas thought was his uncle, but discovered was his father . . . hey, this is a soap, remember?) For a long time, Lucky resented having this big brother just shoved into his life. But now the two guys are trying to bond. It certainly didn't help that Nikolas is a Cassidine, since the Cassidines are lifelong enemies of the Spencers.

Jonathan's relationship with his real-life older brother, Richard Lee Jackson, is a lot more normal. Although Jonathan was born in Orlando, Florida, the boys grew up in the state of Washington, and for the first thirteen years of his life, Jonathan split a room with Richard. You can get pretty tight with someone when you share bunk beds for that long!

You can also get pretty competitive—especially in sports. "When Jon and I were younger, we definitely had a rivalry," Richard admits.

"At first we just wanted to beat each other, then we started to play sports together instead of against each other," Jonathan explains. "We started to see what a good team we could make."

One thing Jonathan and Richard have never competed for were roles. The brothers are phenomenally supportive of one another in their careers. In fact, it was Richard's acting that first brought Jonathan to California.

California Here We Come

In 1991, the Jackson family took a vacation trip to the Universal Studios Hollywood theme park in California. Jonathan and Richard were very intrigued by all of the backstage info they learned at the studio. They decided there and then to become actors. ("Before that I always wanted to be a basketball or baseball player," Jonathan admits.)

When they returned from the vacation, the boys hung together to watch their favorite movies—usually those starring Christian Slater or James Dean. While they watched, they would say the lines with the TV. Eventually, Jonathan and Richard learned to use tape machines to dub their own voices into the films.

"We got addicted to it," Jonathan recalls. "We'd loop our voices over scenes from *Rebel Without a*

Cause and *East of Eden*. My sister [Candice] did Meg Ryan's voice in *When Harry Met Sally*. It was pretty weird."

It was also good training. In 1993, little more than a year after that fateful family vacation, Richard found himself a manager and moved down to Los Angeles in the middle of the school year to pursue his career. Jonathan stayed in Washington with his mom, dad, and sister, taking acting classes. Finally, when the school year came to a close, Jeanine moved Jonathan and Candice to Los Angeles. Jonathan's dad stayed in Washington, but spent time with his wife and kids on weekends. To make sure Jonathan, Richard, and Candice got to "see" their dad as often as possible, Jeanine bought a set of videophones.

Before long, Richard landed a regular role on a show called *Saved by the Bell: The New Class*. Candice did a pilot for a Fox-TV show called *Medicine Ball*, and Jonathan got cast in some commercials.

Jonathan's first ad was for a local grocery chain called Albertsons. Later on, he hawked Happy Meals for McDonald's and made sure he got his pops in a Kellogg's Corn Pops commercial. He was also an extra in the movie *Free Willy*.

Then came the call Jonathan had been waiting for. His manager wanted him to audition for the role of Lucas Lorenzo Spencer Jr. on the soap opera *General Hospital*. It was the first major part Jonathan had ever tried out for. The chances weren't great that he would get the part. After all, plenty of more experienced kids were auditioning for the role. But, we guess you could say Jonathan got Lucky. (Pun intended, of course!)

Life in Port Charles

On October 29, 1993, *GH* fans got their first look at Luke and Laura's eldest offspring. He was the heir apparent to TV's reigning royal family, the Spencers.

Tony Geary and Genie Francis, who play Luke and Laura, are perhaps the most famous performers in the whole history of soap operas. Luke and Laura's wedding ceremony in 1980 was one of the most watched programs of all time. They made the cover of many national magazines and became part of the national consciousness forever. So you might think that Jonathan was a little out of his league going on screen with those two.

But according to Tony Geary, nothing could be further from the truth. "Jonathan is one of the truest actors I have ever worked with," Tony says. "He's a total peer when we work . . . He's the perfect physicalization of Luke and Laura's love. He's a beautiful little guy and he's a great actor who has a wonderful heart."

Pretty high praise, huh? But Tony has gone one step further. He has said that if Jonathan ever decides to leave the cast of *General Hospital*, Tony hopes that the writers will kill off the character of Lucky, rather than recast the role with another actor.

Jonathan is proud of the work he has done with Tony and Genie. He gives them a lot of the credit for his acting success. "I have learned so much from working with both of them," he says thankfully.

Jonathan has also developed his own system for acting. "The basic method I use is talking myself into a scene," he says. "I work at believing the lines like the truth. If you say something to yourself enough, you start to believe it. Once it becomes a reality, it's easy to play."

Jonathan's method works. And the proof wasn't long in coming. In 1995, he won his first Emmy award, for Outstanding Young Actor. Fittingly, Tony and Genie were on the stage to present the award to their TV son.

"It's a hard feeling to express," Jonathan says of that first Emmy win. "Mostly I felt overwhelmed. The best part was having Tony Geary and Genie Francis be the ones to present me with the award."

Jonathan got to experience the thrill of winning an Emmy again in 1998. Once again he made that long trip to the stage, and picked up the golden statue for Outstanding Young Actor.

Making Movies

Each day the cast of *General Hospital* tapes seventy pages of dialogue. Jonathan is a leading player, so he has a lot of memorizing to do. On top of that, he's tutored on the set and by law has to keep up with his schoolwork. It would seem that Jonathan would have little time for anything else.

But Jonathan is busy taking his career to the next level by making movies. His first film was released back in 1994. He played Morris "Mud" Himmel in a movie called *Camp Nowhere*.

Although Jonathan had only spent one week of his life at summer camp ("It was called Camp Big Lake. It was fun. I had a pretty good time," he recalls), he loved playing the role of a smart kid who comes up with a plan to create a camp that's actually run by kids. The movie was a total comedy, which was a nice switch from Lucky's angst-ridden life. Jonathan enjoyed being part of the on-camera food fights and mud romps. It was also good for Jonathan to be part of a cast that was made up primarily of kids. He still keeps up with some of his cast mates.

Jonathan liked the slower pace of moviemaking.

Soap opera episodes are filmed daily. There isn't much time for rehearsal or experimentation. Movies take their time.

"I really like the [movie] medium," Jonathan says. "It's much slower paced and relaxed, and you have much more time to work on what you are doing."

Jonathan had a chance to work in the movie medium again in 1996, when he played Matt Rainie in the made-for-TV movie, *The Legend of the Ruby Silver*. Jonathan costarred with *Dukes of Hazzard* alum John Schneider in this story of four lost souls who go in search of the bloodred silver found only in the Ruby Silver Mine. Later that same year Jonathan played two roles in *Prisoner of Zenda*, another made-for-TV movie which starred *Star Trek*'s Captain Kirk, William Shatner. It was Jonathan's performance in that film which most impressed Tony Geary.

"He did a movie on Showtime, *Prisoner of Zenda*, where he played two characters, and neither one was like Lucky," Tony told *Soap Opera Digest* in 1996. "I was worried for a while that he was absorbing too much of the two of us [Genie Francis and himself]. But he isn't, and I'm pleased to see that."

Tony hadn't seen anything yet. Jonathan's most challenging non-Lucky role was yet to come.

☆ Sizzlin' Soap Stars ☆

The Deep End of the Ocean

You might call 1996 the year of Oprah Winfrey's book club. That year the popular daytime talk show host began recommending books for her audience to read. The first book on her list was Jacquelyn Mitchard's *The Deep End of the Ocean*—a story of the family left behind when a small boy is kidnapped.

Oprah's seal of approval was all *The Deep End of the Ocean* needed to propel it to number one on the *New York Times* bestseller list. After that, Hollywood came calling. Michelle Pfeiffer desperately wanted to play the character of Beth Cappadora, the happily married mother whose life is turned upside down when her son Ben disappears. Treat Williams and Whoopi Goldberg were quickly tapped to play the other adult leading roles. But one problem remained. What actor could portray Vincent, the son who was left behind? The actor had to be versatile enough to play Vincent at both age thirteen and age seventeen. He had to be able to convey great fear, sorrow, and anger. And he had to be hunky enough for audiences to believe that the gorgeous Michelle Pfeiffer was his mother.

Sound like anyone you know?

Sure enough, Jonathan got the part. Once again, he was able to hold his own against some of the entertainment industry's most formidable actors. In fact, Jonathan's performance was so intensely brilliant that even before the film's release in February 1999, industry insiders were linking Jonathan's name to the Oscars.

"Leo Schmeo," *TV Guide* said in its June 13, 1998, Summer Soaps Preview. "We predict sixteen-year-old Jonathan Jackson . . . will soon be stealing thunder from titanic DiCaprio. Movie makers clearly think so: Jackson's already generating Oscar buzz for his performance of Michelle Pfeiffer's tormented son in the film version of Jacqueline Mitchard's *The Deep End of the Ocean*."

Will *TV Guide*'s prediction ring true? Only time will tell. But one thing is for sure, the comparisons to that other blond-haired hottie are coming quick and furious. So how does Jonathan feel about the comparisons to Leonardo DiCaprio?

"It's flattering," he says, "but it's getting a little old."

Maybe so, but if the ocean can do for Jonathan's career what it did for Leo's, no one will be complaining!

What Does the Future Hold?

Now that he's getting rave reviews for his big-screen performance, will Jonathan be joining other small-screen actors in teen movies? Not likely. According to Jonathan, *The Deep End of the Ocean* is a fluke. "There aren't a lot of movie roles for people my age—not good ones anyway," he told *TV Guide*. "*Scream* is not where my strength is."

And if Jonathan has any say, you won't be seeing him in any steamy love scenes like the ones Brenda and Jax used to have, either. You see, Jonathan is a devout Christian, and he has some problems with that kind of on-screen passion.

"Luckily, I haven't had a conflict with the sex stuff yet," he explains. "I don't know how I'm going to deal with that. It contradicts what I believe. But I have to keep in mind that I'm not Lucky and and I can't make a living doing Christian projects.

"I would just hope the producers would talk to me about it first," he adds. "I am sure I could protest to ensure the decency of how it's done."

Although Jonathan has ruled out being on any other soaps in the future ("*General Hospital* is too much like home for me to go on to any other soap opera," he explains), he did have a good time guest-starring on the prime-time sitcom *Boy Meets World* last year. Jonathan played a young, handsome, sensitive American artist who had studied in Paris and come home to the States. (Is it any wonder people keep comparing Jonathan to Leo?!) Jonathan enjoyed the experience and says starring in a sitcom might be fun someday, although he has no immediate plans to do one.

In the meantime, Jonathan is spending his spare time playing guitar for his rock band, Scarlet Road. Scarlet Road is strictly a Jackson family affair. Jonathan writes the music and lyrics, plays lead guitar, and sings. Jonathan's brother, Richard, plays drums, his dad, Ricky Lee, is on bass and vocals, and his uncle Gary sings backup. Scarlet Road was originally the name of a garage band Jonathan's dad and uncle had in the 1960s. That Scarlet Road went nowhere. But this new incarnation of the band has recorded a CD, *CLASH*, which you can buy over the Internet. (Just in case you were wondering, that *is* Jonathan singing and playing the guitar on *General Hospital*.)

As if that weren't enough, Jonathan and Richard have teamed up again. But this time, it's not for sports. The brothers have just completed their first screenplay, and are getting ready to shop it around to the studios.

While acting may have been Richard's idea first, it was Jonathan who first took to the computer keyboard to write the script. "I had to convince Richard [to try writing]," Jonathan claims. "I said, 'You can do this.' He dragged his feet, but finally said, 'Fine!' We wrote the story outline and then he took over and became the head writer."

Wow! Acting, playing music, writing . . . there seems to be no stopping the brothers Jackson! And that's just fine with Jonathan. After all, his brother is his best friend now. "We're still around the same people, we do the same things, we have common interests and common goals," Jonathan says of his relationship with Richard. "We're going down the road together."

☆ Jonathan Jackson ☆
Fast Facts

Birthday: May 11
Hair Color: Dark blond
Eyes: Blue
Height: 5'7" (But he's still growing!)
Favorite Sports: Basketball and baseball
Favorite Color: Blue
Favorite Car: Porsche
Pets: Five cats: Misty, Meow, Smokey, Shadow, and Studmuffin
Favorite Musical Group: U2
Favorite TV Show: *Friends*
Most Prized Possession: Life

Tyler Christopher
(Jon McKee/Retna)

Alison Sweeney
(Steve Granitz/Retna)

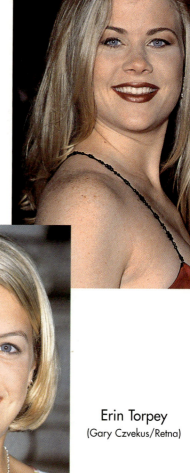

Erin Torpey
(Gary Czvekus/Retna)

Jonathan Jackson
(Walter McBride/Retna)

Vanessa Marcil
(Jon McKee/Retna)

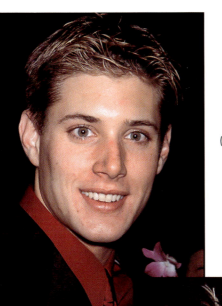

Jensen Ackles
(Walter McBride/Retna)

Jacob Young
(Steve Granitz/Retna)

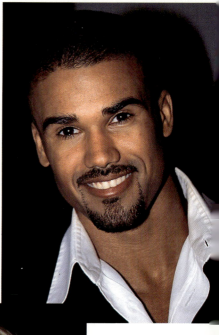

Shemar Moore
(Joseph Marzullo/Retna)

Adrienne Frantz
(Steve Granitz/Retna)

Steve Burton
(Jon McKee/Retna)

Vanessa Marcil,
Alison Sweeney,
and Adrienne Frantz
(Jon McKee/Retna)

Rebecca Herbst
(Steve Granitz/Retna)

7

Vanessa Marcil

(ex–Brenda Barrett, *General Hospital*)

When Vanessa Marcil was a kid, her favorite soap opera was *General Hospital*. In fact, one of her clearest childhood memories is the day she met Anthony Geary (Luke) for the first time.

"I remember when I was about eleven years old, and Tony Geary came to the Palm Springs Mall to sign autographs. I stood in line for hours and when I finally met him, I cried."

Unfortunately, memories are all Vanessa has of that meeting. The photos her mother took of Vanessa and Tony were stolen before the roll of film was ever developed.

These days, fans wait in line for hours to meet Vanessa, and she is always kind because she remembers what it was like to be one of them.

"I have so many fans who support me no matter what," she says gratefully. "I love meeting them. But I don't want them to ever believe that I'm any different than they are. We all want the same thing. We just want to be normal and have a family."

Maybe so, but there *is* something special about Vanessa. She has a star quality that everyone—from the Artist Formerly Known as Prince to the fans on the street—can't help but notice.

Growing up Can Be Hard

Perhaps the young Vanessa was so obsessed with the trials and tribulations of *General Hospital*'s characters because her own life was a lot less than perfect.

Vanessa is the youngest of the four children in her family. She has two older sisters, Tina and Sherry, and an older brother, Sam. Although Vanessa was born in hot, hot Palm Springs, her father, contractor Peter Ortiz (Marcil is actually Vanessa's mother, Patricia's, maiden name), soon moved the whole family to cold, cold Anchorage, Alaska. But the change in weather was the least of Vanessa's problems.

"I was young; her father was young," Patricia once revealed to *Soap Opera World* about Vanessa's early childhood. "It was children raising children."

And that, as any soap opera fan knows, is a recipe for disaster.

Unfortunately for Vanessa, her childhood was

no television show. It was real life. And, according to Vanessa, it was very sad. As she once told *Soap Opera Digest*, Vanessa's father had some major problems.

"I was so angry at him for so long," she told the magazine. "He was very abusive—physically and emotionally." She added, "I was not allowed to express myself when I was a kid."

Those kinds of problems can take their toll—especially on someone as intensely sensitive as Vanessa. Luckily, she did have one place where she was free from the turmoil she found at home. When Vanessa was about eight, the family moved back to California. That's when Vanessa's mother introduced her daughter to the world of the theater.

"My mother understood early on that I wanted to be an actress. I remember very clearly the first time she brought me to the Children's Circle Theater in Palm Springs. I knew then and there that was exactly what I wanted to do."

Once she discovered the theater, she pursued her passion in true Vanessa fashion. She read everything she could about actors and actresses. She studied great plays, and began performing in local amateur groups. In sixth grade she won a talent show by playing the guitar and singing a song she'd written by herself.

But even the theater world couldn't heal all of

Vanessa's wounds, and eventually, as a teenager, she began to drown her sorrows in alcohol.

Although she's been clean and sober for more than eight years now (a fact she is very proud of!), Vanessa has never forgotten the trouble alcohol got her into as a teen.

"I can't tell you how many times as a child I was written off as a bad kid," she told *Soap Opera Weekly*. "Everyone needs someone to be there for them."

In Vanessa's case, the person who was there for her was none other than the Artist Formerly Known as Prince.

"I became friendly with Prince before I got into acting. I think it was meant to be, because he believed in me at a time when I really needed that. I was just a small-town kid from Palm Springs with a drinking problem and bad grades, and he was someone [whose picture] I had on the wall in my room," she recalls.

The Artist asked Vanessa to dance at a club, and the two became friends. Years later, he asked Vanessa to perform in videos for the songs "The Most Beautiful Girl in the World" (a title many fans have given her as well) and "Undertaker."

But the Artist gave Vanessa more than just a leg up in the entertainment business. He also taught her a very valuable lesson.

"I realized that the only reason for fame is to help people," she says. "Because [the Artist] was so much bigger than life, I believed him. It doesn't really make sense, but it is a reality in this world. I'm no better than someone who isn't an actor, but for some reason kids will listen to me. I can use this to an advantage by only telling people positive things."

A Las Vegas Wedding

The Artist Formerly Known as Prince wasn't the only celebrity Vanessa met while she was just starting out. In the summer of 1989, Vanessa was quietly eating lunch at one of her favorite vegetarian restaurants when she met Corey Feldman. Corey was a successful actor at the time, but he had a big drug and alcohol problem. He and Vanessa became fast friends.

"We were two people with a need for someone to love us," Corey told *People* magazine.

After only two months, Vanessa accompanied Corey on a movie publicity trip to Las Vegas. While they were there, they decided to have a spur-of-the-moment wedding.

In the past, Vanessa has said that the wedding was really just a joke: she and Corey didn't even use their real names, and they never even lived in the same house. So you can imagine how surprised Vanessa was when she found out that they actually had to get the marriage *legally* dissolved.

But even if the wedding was a joke, the friendship wasn't. Vanessa knew that Corey needed her help. His drug use was getting worse and worse. So Vanessa helped convince him to check into a rehab center. She even joined him in some of his therapy sessions. Today, like Vanessa, Corey is clean and sober.

Vanessa Marcil, Legal Eagle

Despite all of her problems, Vanessa was a smart girl. She'd even skipped a year in grade school. So when she went to college, Vanessa picked one of the toughest subjects to major in—prelaw. Vanessa felt it wasn't that big a leap from acting to law. She figured that most lawyers are actors anyway. And besides, she knew she could convince almost anyone to see things her way.

But eventually the lure of the stage proved greater than the lure of the courtroom. Vanessa found herself going back to perform in community theater. She got herself a manager and took roles in amateur productions of plays like *Cat on a Hot Tin Roof*, *Pygmalion*, *Mamet's Women*, and *Sweet Bird of Youth* while she waited for her big break.

Like many other undiscovered actresses, Vanessa worked odd jobs to pay the bills. Her last job before landing the role of Brenda on *General Hospital* was at a fast-food joint called The Wiener Schnitzel. "I was the French-fry girl," she remembers. "I wore a polyester, brown-and-orange, really hideous outfit."

The Wiener Schnitzel didn't exactly offer a six-figure salary, so Vanessa shared a one-room apartment with three other girls. Ironically, she remembers those times as being a lot of fun.

"My friends and I would go buy a bag of potatoes and try and figure out all kinds of ways to make them," she recalls with a laugh. "We were just kids, hanging out, living dirty and cheap.

"I'm glad that I started that way, because it keeps me really grateful and humble about everything," she adds with her characteristic optimism.

Becoming Brenda

Vanessa auditioned for the role of *General Hospital*'s deceitful vixen, Brenda Barrett, in the spring of 1992. She'd never had a professional role before, so she didn't have high hopes for getting the part. But Vanessa really liked the character. Brenda was devious, sneaky, and sensuous. The kind of role actresses love to sink their teeth into.

Vanessa wanted that part—bad! So bad, that not even doughnuts could calm her stressed-out nerves.

"After I auditioned for the part it was days before I heard I'd gotten it," Vanessa recalls. "So while I waited, I ate. That's what I do when I worry, I eat. I must have called my agent from every restaurant in Hollywood. It was constantly, 'Have you heard yet? Have you heard yet?'

"Finally I drove up to a pay phone and called, and got the good news. I started crying right there on the curb. People must have thought I was crazy until I starting shouting, 'I just got *General Hospital!*'"

Only in Hollywood, right?

On September 18, 1992, Brenda Barrett made her first appearance on *General Hospital*. She was a gorgeous boarding school dropout who had come to live in Port Charles with her big sister Julia. From the moment she arrived in town Brenda had her eye on Jagger Cates. She would stop at nothing to keep him from his true love, Karen Wexler.

Ordinarily, the character of Brenda would be just the kind of girl audiences love to hate. But something strange happened with the role. Audiences actually *loved* Brenda. They rooted for her! According to *General Hospital* head writer Bob

☆ Sizzlin' Soap Stars ☆

Guza, that's a credit to Vanessa's natural acting ability.

"She has an extremely unique capacity to project simultaneous strength and vulnerability," Bob explains. "So even when you see her collapsing, you see a strong woman collapsing. When she's giving herself, you see a strong independent woman giving herself. That's very hard to find, but she has it."

While Vanessa was a popular actress during those Brenda/Jagger days, it wasn't until 1993, when the *GH* writers introduced a shady mob boss named Sonny Corinthos, that Vanessa's popularity soared to the cosmos.

Sonny and Brenda were *General Hospital*'s most beloved couple. Their faces were plastered on the covers of magazines, on bus stops, and on billboards . Women everywhere wanted that "Brenda" look. Even *Vogue* magazine photographed some of their models posing with their sweater sleeves pulled over their hands—just the way Vanessa does. (The thing is, Vanessa doesn't do that to make a fashion statement. She's anemic, and pulling the sleeves over her hands helps keep her warm!)

ABC knew it had a megastar on its hands. So in 1994 the network asked Vanessa to host its late-night show, *ABC In Concert*. It was an opportunity Vanessa could not give up—even though it meant flying six thousand miles round trip every weekend. (*General Hospital* tapes in L.A., and *In Concert* came out of New York.)

Vanessa loved New York. She got an apartment with a friend and stayed there on the weekends. The city provided Vanessa with a brand-new dream. "Someday I would love to sing in a show on Broadway," she admitted at the time. It's a goal she's still hanging on to. And knowing Vanessa, you'll probably see her there. This girl knows how to get what she wants!

Eventually, the *In Concert* gig came to an end. But Vanessa's popularity kept growing. In 1995 *People* magazine voted her one of the fifty most beautiful people in the world. And in May 1997 she was nominated for her first daytime Emmy award in the Best Supporting Actress category.

Making It in the Movies

As Vanessa's popularity grew, the offers started piling up at her agent's office. There were chances to be part of films like *Race the Sun* and *Don Juan DeMarco*, but Vanessa's busy GH schedule forced her to give them up. Not being able to do *Don Juan DeMarco* was especially hard for her, because the movie starred her all-time acting hero, Marlon Brando.

"It did break my heart that I couldn't do it," Vanessa recalls, "but I believe there's a higher power who has everything going on for one reason or another. It's scary to let something go that's good, but I think that's part of the lesson. You have to know your self-worth and that you can let good things go and let new things come."

And new things—*great things*—did come. In 1996, she auditioned for the part of Nicolas Cage's girlfriend in *The Rock*. It was a tough audition.

"[The audition script] was three pages long and in that one scene my character started out singing a Country-Western song, then spoke with a New Jersey accent, then switched to a Western accent, then burst into tears," she says. "I was like, 'Excuse me, but I'm not going to do all that unless I'm getting paid.' I thought it was a pretty large bill to fill for an audition scene."

Maybe so, but it was a bill Vanessa could fill. She got the part. And this time *General Hospital* Executive Producer Wendy Riche juggled Vanessa's soap schedule so she could take the role. For several weeks, Vanessa spent her time jetting back and forth from GH's Los Angeles studio to *The Rock*'s San Francisco set.

The Rock introduced Vanessa to a wider audience, and before long offers were flying in fast and furious. Wendy Riche agreed to another schedule juggling act in late 1996, so Vanessa could take on her first starring role in the made-for-TV movie *To Love, Honor and Deceive*.

In *To Love, Honor and Deceive*, Vanessa played a wife and mother whose life is devastated when her husband and son are presumed dead following a boating accident. But things go from bad to worse when she discovers that her husband faked his death and kidnapped his son. *To Love, Honor and Deceive* got mixed reviews, but Vanessa's personal notices were great. Better still, the ratings were huge. Vanessa's star was rising higher than ever!

Ties with Tyler

Brenda Barrett has had her share of romantic leading men. At one point she was in love with two of them at the same time—Sonny Corinthos and Jasper Jacks. But there's only one love in *Vanessa's* life. He's Tyler Christopher, who plays Nikolas Cassidine on *GH*. The two met back in 1996, on Tyler's first day of work. Vanessa came over and introduced herself so Tyler wouldn't feel out of place or lonely.

Romance didn't happen right away. In fact, it took that slow pace soap operas are famous for. When the two first met, Tyler had a girlfriend, and Vanessa was involved with Nathan Fillion, who played Joey Buchanan on *One Life to Live*.

☆ Sizzlin' Soap Stars ☆

But within a few months, both Vanessa and Tyler had broken off their relationships. And when Tyler visited Vanessa on the North Carolina set of *To Love, Honor and Deceive*, there was no denying it. The friendship had definitely blossomed into something more.

Vanessa and Tyler eventually became engaged. Deciding to marry Tyler was not the only big decision Vanessa had to make in 1997. Her contract with *General Hospital* was coming to an end. Her agents and managers were begging her to leave the soap opera, and try her luck at a big-screen or prime-time TV career. But Vanessa was happy playing Brenda. The writers were giving her brilliant story lines—like overcoming a prescription drug addiction. And there was the added incentive of having Tyler on the set every day.

Finally, Vanessa made a very controversial decision. She opted to stay on *General Hospital* for a while. "I just wanted to be challenged in my acting," she explains. "I don't really care about becoming a big star. That may be hard for some people to believe."

Her agents sure didn't believe it. They almost dropped Vanessa as a client when she signed on to do more work on *General Hospital*. But even they had to admit that Vanessa had some extraordinary story lines to play in 1998. The writers gave Brenda a nervous breakdown when Sonny left her standing at the altar. The performance earned Vanessa her second Emmy nomination, an honor made even sweeter because Tyler was also nominated.

Finally, though, in late 1998, Vanessa made the difficult break from the cast and crew of *General Hospital*. Her last story line was wild! The writers arranged for Brenda's mother to come back to town. Brenda's mom had a debilitating brain disease that was slowly making her insane, and the disease was hereditary! Had Brenda inherited the gene for the disease? Viewers never found out, because Brenda and her mother eventually drove off a cliff to their (supposed) deaths. But, in true soap opera fashion, their bodies were never found, leaving the door open for a return of Brenda in the future.

After leaving Port Charles, Vanessa moved on to a much ritzier zip code. Soon after her last appearance as Brenda, Vanessa made her first appearance as Gina on Fox's prime-time soap, *Beverly Hills 90210*. Gina was a true soap opera villain—an ice skater with a heart as cold as the ice she skated on.

What's Next for Vanessa?

Leaving Port Charles wasn't easy for Vanessa, but luckily she's still tightly tied to the *General*

Hospital family. After all, she's marrying the crown prince of the Cassidines. Tyler and Vanessa's wedding was originally supposed to take place last December, but Vanessa was suddenly offered a starring role in an upcoming Disney movie called *A Matter of Trust*. So she and Tyler agreed to delay the ceremony.

The delay actually pleased one of the couple's good friends. "At least now I have time to save up for a wedding present," Steve Burton (Jason Morgan on *General Hospital*) joked to *Soap Opera Update*.

But Vanessa's and Tyler's fans saw the postponement as a danger sign. Rumors of a breakup spread like wildfire across the Internet.

"I heard that I broke up with Tyler and that he and Ingo [Rademacher, who plays Jax] got into a fight in the parking lot. It's hysterical. Our real lives are so boring that I guess it's disappointing to people," Vanessa sighs.

The truth is, Tyler and Vanessa are still happily together and waiting for a break in their schedules so they can get married. "The reality is we truly want a great honeymoon," Vanessa explains. "It's hard with our schedules to get two weeks off at the same time."

And it's getting more difficult every day. In addition to *Beverly Hills 90210* and *A Matter of Trust*, Vanessa has also just wrapped two independent projects, *The Space Between Us* and *Nice Guys Sleep Alone*. She's also looking at more scripts, and she longs to do stage work again.

But no matter how busy Vanessa gets, both she and Tyler find time for their charity work. Vanessa spends a lot of her free time with abused and underprivileged children.

"I try to teach them to have self-esteem because that's what gets taken from you when you're abused. Nothing is as important as a child in need of help," she declares.

Vanessa has set up a charity with proceeds benefiting the Sojourn House for battered women and their children. Recently she and Tyler hosted a charity ball for Sojourn House. They raised more than fifteen thousand dollars.

So with a wedding to plan, charity events to sponsor, and a new prime-time job, how does Vanessa plan to spend her few precious free hours in the upcoming months? Shopping! She and Tyler have just bought a house, and they need to decorate.

"It's a cute, three-story, turn-of-the-century home with fireplaces and hardwood floors," Vanessa reveals.

It's also empty. Neither Vanessa nor Tyler had much furniture before they bought the house.

"Before this, I lived with three other girls, and Tyler lived with four other guys, in bachelor and bachelorette pads. So between the two of us, we own nothing," she laughs.

Sounds like the perfect opportunity to fill the house with beautiful things . . . and someday, with a few kids.

"My dream is that I want to have a family," she says.

Dreams have a way of coming true for Vanessa. Maybe that's why, despite all the hard times, these days Vanessa's life seems to be more of a fairy tale than a soap opera. After all, she and Tyler are achieving something no soap opera couple can ever do—they are living happily ever after.

☆ Vanessa Marcil ☆
Fast Facts

Birthday: October 15
Height: 5'4"
Hair: Brown
Eyes: Brown
Pets: Two dogs, Woof and Joey
Hobbies: Riding motorcycles, singing, seeing movies with friends
Favorite Musical Artist: The Artist Formerly Known as Prince
Favorite Movie: *Grease*
Favorite Drink: Chinese herbal tonic
Professional Dream: "I'd love to shave my head and do a weird film where I'm in an insane asylum and I don't have to be the pretty girl."
Tattoo: Vanessa has an Egyptian tribal-design tattoo. It is a symbol that means love and peace in the universe.

Shemar Moore

(Malcolm Winters, *The Young and the Restless*)

You might not think of mighty, muscular Shemar Moore as a real mama's boy, but that's exactly how this hottie thinks of himself. And as far Shemar's concerned, there's nothing wrong with that. In fact, he's proud of his devotion to his mom. After all, Shemar knows that a lot of the credit for his current success goes to his mom.

"My mother sacrificed a lot," he explains. "I have to thank my mother for this journey to success. All the sacrifices she made in life led me to have the opportunities I have today. She kept things in perspective. She gave me reality checks."

Keeping things in perspective wasn't always easy, partially because of the reactions some people had to his parents' marriage. Shemar's mother, Marilyn, is white, and his father, Sherrod, is black.

"They believed that their love was what was real," Shemar says of his 'rents. "It didn't matter about color. You could mesh and there could be harmony. They wanted their child to be a product of [those beliefs], so they took the first three letters of their names—She-Mar—and that's me."

Shemar's parents were dedicated to making sure their son was kept as far as possible from racist attitudes. But that wasn't easy in the United States during the late 1960s. So, soon after baby Shemar's birth, the Moores moved to Denmark, where they hoped people would be more open-minded about their family.

Denmark did provide Shemar with a haven from racism, but it couldn't protect him from the troubles that had started to form in his parents' marriage. By the time Shemar was three, his parents had divorced. And while Shemar says his dad "sort of drifted in and out of the picture," Shemar's mom dedicated her life to her son's physical and mental well-being.

"There has always been a strong sense of harmony within my family structure," Shemar says of his life with his mother. "My mother made it apparent in how I was taken care of and shown support. She taught me to believe in myself and not think I was different because I wasn't of one race. That's my whole thing. I know I can't save the world, but I can stand on that sense of integrity—treating all as equal."

About a year after his parents' divorce, Shemar and his mother moved to Bahrain, a country in the Persian Gulf. Marilyn taught school in Bahrain for two years. Then she decided to return to the United States. So she and Shemar moved to Boston, Marilyn's hometown.

For the first time, Shemar was faced with racism. "It was a complete culture shock for me," he says of his years in Massachusetts.

Eventually the racism got so intense that once again the ever protective Marilyn moved her son away from the trouble. They finally settled in Palo Alto, California.

Palo Alto was a good place for Shemar. In high school he developed into a total jock, making the baseball team. The combination of that varsity letter and his exotic, muscular good looks turned Shemar into quite the ladies' man. Girls from freshmen to seniors were suddenly hanging on his every word and clamoring for dates with him. Let's face it, no man can avoid falling for that kind of flattery! Shemar hit the dating scene, big time!

The attention and popularity were definitely great, but Shemar's grades were starting to fall. So, once again, mama Marilyn stepped in. She used what Shemar calls "tough love" to get her son's grades back up. Basically it came down to "no grades, no baseball."

The technique worked. By his senior year, Shemar's grades were good enough to get him into Santa Clara University, and his baseball skills were so great that he managed to score a partial scholarship!

Say Cheese, Shemar!

A partial scholarship is a great thing. But Shemar needed to find a way to pay the *rest* of his tuition. So he decided to put his looks to good use and try modeling. After all, everyone in high school thought he was good looking. And although that's never been important to Shemar—"You can call me a hunk all day long and compliment me left and right, but what means the most to me is that people feel I'm approachable," he says—he knew that modeling paid well.

A modeling agency called City Models took one look at Shemar's pics (and pecs) and signed him to a contract. Before long, Shemar's handsome image was gracing fashion layouts in *Gentleman's Quarterly* and *Mademoiselle*. He also strutted the runways for some major designers.

Modeling eventually led to TV commercials. Shemar became a featured actor in ads for McDonalds, Levi jeans, Miller beer, and Cotler clothes.

By the time Shemar finished his studies he had a very impressive portfolio. He also had something far more important—his diploma, with a degree in communications.

"I wouldn't have this type of success if I hadn't graduated," he says. "A degree shows the world you can complete a project . . . you can stick it out and take direction. You can pay your dues."

The Graduate

After college, Shemar tried harder to break into acting. He went to auditions and found small guest-star roles on shows such as *Living Single* and *Arli$$—The Art of the Super Sports Agent*. But there was nothing steady about the work, and the pay was less than spectacular. So Shemar kept up with his modeling.

Ironically it was the modeling that led him to his biggest role yet. In 1994, the producers of *The Young and the Restless* were looking for someone to play the younger brother of Neil Winters (played by Kristoff St. John). They called veteran Hollywood casting agent Sid Craig, and asked him if he had any clients who might fit the bill. He didn't. But Sid's not the type of man who gives up easily. He agreed to look around and see if he could find anyone hunky enough for the role. While looking through an issue of *Gentleman's Quarterly*, Sid happened on Shemar's picture. He called the magazine, got Shemar's number, and the rest, as they say, is history.

Even though his modeling career did lead him

to the *Y&R* audition, Shemar wants his fans to know that it wasn't just his looks that got him the role on *The Young and the Restless*.

"I don't want people to think that because I was a pretty face, I got the part," he insists. "There's a lot of reasons why I had the opportunity. I was prepared. And I continue to study to this day."

Shemar was not always so confident about his acting skills. In fact, he was sure he was going to get fired on his first day on *The Young and the Restless* set.

"I was a model, just out of college," he explains. "I thought, 'What if they see through me?'"

But all the cast and producers of *The Young and the Restless* saw was a talented and dedicated young man who was working hard to hone his craft.

"Within two days he was in acting class," Shemar's costar Tonya Lee Williams (Olivia) says. "He got real serious and never let up."

Shemar quickly discovered some of the perks of stardom, namely, Hollywood starlets. He has been linked with some of the most beautiful women in town. For instance, Shemar met Toni Braxton while working on her video "How Many Ways."

"We had a little bit of chemistry and a little bit of curiosity," he laughs.

But the chemistry wasn't as strong as Shemar might have hoped. He and Toni split up after a few months. In 1996, when he met Halle Berry on the

CBS lot (she was filming *Bulworth*), he dropped a few hints that they should keep in touch... which they did. Unfortunately that relationship ended after about a year.

Which leaves Shemar a free man at the moment. Any takers?

Feeling Young and Restless

Malcolm Winters is an interesting soap opera character. He started out as someone Shemar's mother definitely would *not* be proud of—remember when he seduced his brother's wife while she was too groggy with cold medicine to refuse? But the character of Malcolm has slowly evolved into less of a bad seed and more of a streetwise rogue with a heart of gold. He's someone so caring that he married the AIDS-stricken Keesha on her deathbed.

"My character is a little bit of street," Shemar says. "But he has that sense of realism, a sense of progress, and a sense of values. He's not just speaking Ebonics."

As far as Shemar is concerned, the real reason for Malcolm's popularity is not Shemar's portrayal of him, but the high caliber of writing on *The Young and the Restless*.

"I think more than anything, the reason [*The*

Young and the Restless] is successful is because of the show's positive images [of African-Amercans]. We can be doctors. We can be lawyers. We can be photographers. It's not inner-city struggle all the time. They don't portray stereotypes: the thugs and gangsters."

It's nice that Malcolm is such a well-rounded character. And the fans do appreciate watching their favorite character grow as a person. But ask any fan what they like best about Shemar, and they are more than likely to tell you it's his muscular body. Maybe that's why *The Young and the Restless* writers include plenty of scenes that feature Shemar without his shirt on. (FYI to fans: Although Shemar is willing to take his shirt off on camera—don't ask him to do it at celebrity events or signings. He never does.)

Because even portraying a character as fully evolved as Malcolm Winters is not enough to satisfy Shemar's acting palate, he's recently taken on some other roles as well. He made a move to CBS prime time for a night, playing a fighter who is beaten to death on *Chicago Hope*. He joined other *The Young and the Restless* and *The Bold and the Beautiful* stars on a special episode of *The Nanny*, and he took on the lead role of Freddy Rowland in HBO's original movie, *Butter*.

Shemar's most profound prime-time role came in November 1998. He played Lincoln Fleming in

Mama Flora's Family, the highly anticipated follow-up to Alex Haley's renowned *Roots*. Shemar demonstrated just how far he'd come as an actor, holding his own with such acclaimed stars as Cicely Tyson, Queen Latifah, Blair Underwood, and Mario Van Peebles.

If you're wondering whether all this means that Shemar will be leaving *The Young and the Restless* anytime soon, relax. Right now he's happy with playing Malcolm, as long as the producers give him time to pursue other projects as well.

Still, he does hope to branch out into primetime TV and movies in a big way someday. That ambition has led some people to call Shemar the next Denzel Washington. But Shemar doesn't see it that way.

"I don't want to be the next Denzel. I want to be the first Shemar Moore," he declares. "Basically I want to get out there and try. If I fall on my butt, at least I know I tried."

Now there's an attitude that's sure to make his mama proud.

☆ Shemar Moore ☆
Fast Facts

Birthday: April 20, 1970
Hair: Black
Eyes: Brown
Height: 6'1"
Nickname: Sham
He Fantasizes About: Having three kids and a beautiful wife
Favorite Car: BMW 850
Pet Peeve: Talking on the phone. "I'd rather see the person face to face."
Favorite Play: *A Raisin in the Sun*
Favorite Book: *The Hobbit*
Favorite Singer: Marvin Gaye
Favorite Ice Cream: Ben & Jerry's Chocolate Chip Cookie Dough
Favorite Color: Forest green

9

Alison Sweeney

(Sami Brady, *Days of Our Lives*)

Remember that day back in January 1993, when sweet, innocent Sami Brady reappeared on *Days of Our Lives* after being gone for so long?

What's that? *Sweet* Sami Brady? Isn't that a weird way to describe a character who in six short years has managed to kidnap her baby sister, change paternity results, drug her boyfriend, shoot and castrate a rapist, and get herself arrested for the murder of her unfaithful fiancé? Well, according to Alison Sweeney, the actress who brings the devious Sami to life each day (and who has won two *Soap Opera Digest* Best Villianess awards for her efforts), Sami wasn't always such a vixen.

"When I started working [on *Days of Our Lives*] Sami was the sweet, good girl from next door," Alison recalls. "It's just that nobody helped her out of situations, and she went down the wrong path."

According to Alison, turning Sami into daytime's most devious diva was always part of the plan.

"I would say [*Days of Our Lives* head writer] Jim Reilly created my character—built my character—to become a villain. He started very methodically from the beginning, creating a background, a reason, for my character to become a villain."

And Ali's not complaining. She actually enjoys playing the bad girl. "Sometimes I think it would be nice to be in [good girl] Carrie's position, but then it's usually fun resetting watches, changing test results, and shooting people," she admits.

Does Ali think that some of Sami's deviant behavior is over the top—even for a soap opera character?

"Considering I'm on the same show as someone who was possessed by the devil and another who buried someone alive, no, I don't think it's unrealistic," she jokes.

Sami isn't the only one to have gone through some major changes since 1993. Alison has gone through quite a few herself.

"I was sixteen when I started the show," she recently told *Soap Opera Digest*. "I wasn't that good, and I was new and young and had all this energy. Now, I'm staggering into work at 6:45 A.M."

Alison's being pretty harsh. Actually she has always been wonderful as Sami. And why wouldn't

☆ Sizzlin' Soap Stars ☆

she be? She's got plenty of acting experience. Alison's been a professional actress since she was just five years old.

Picture Perfect

Say cheese! That's a sentence lots of kids hear all the time, when their proud parents snap photos. But Alison was actually the kid on the Kodak camera *commercial*.

"My mom thought it would be cute if I was in commercials," Alison recalls. "And I loved doing it."

Alison wanted more than just to be a cute kid who smiled for the cameras. She wanted to be a true actress. And so, from a very young age, she took acting classes to help her develop her technique.

Those classes paid off. At age six, she made her first *Days of Our Lives* appearance. But not as Sami. Alison played Adrienne as a child in two flashback sequences. It was a small part, and not one that people necessarily remember. In fact, years later, even the *Days* casting people were surprised to hear about it.

If you had seen Alison on *Days* back then, you wouldn't recognize her either. For one thing, little Ali had short, short hair. She started to grow it out when she was about seven, and she's had that long beautiful blond mane ever since. (A word to the wise: Alison says the secret to her luxurious hair is lots and lots of conditioner!)

As a child actress, Alison's days were often spent on the sets of hit television shows. She guest-starred on shows like *Simon & Simon*, *Webster*, *Saint Elsewhere*, *Family Man*, *Brand New Life*, *I Married Dora*, and *Tales from the Darkside*.

But through it all, Alison managed to have friends and go to a normal school. In fact, she was actually in her high school math class when she got the call that she had been cast as Sami on *Days of Our Lives*. That one phone call changed the days of Alison's life forever!

Welcome to Salem

"I was like, 'Oh my God, *Days of Our Lives!*'" Alison recalls her early impressions of her new job. "Looking back now, I can admit it was the thrill of my job that kept me working at it."

And the job *was* thrilling! From the very beginning, Alison had the opportunity to work with some of the greatest soap opera actors around, including Deidre Hall (who plays Sami's mom, Marlena), Wayne Northrop (ex-Roman), and Drake Hogestyn (John).

"I've always been very lucky," Alison eagerly admits. "I've gotten the chance to work with a lot

☆ Sizzlin' Soap Stars ☆

of different people. I feel really lucky because I'm not hunkered down to one other cast member."

But taking on such a central role did take its toll on the sixteen-year-old girl. Suddenly she had pages of dialogue to learn, in addition to her school work. But Alison was determined, and she graduated from high school on time. She even brought fellow cast mate Bryan Dattilo (Lucas) to her senior prom.

Once she graduated from high school, you might think that Alison would call it quits for a while on the school thing. After all, college will always be there, right? *Wrong!* College has always been a dream of Alison's. And anyone who knows Ali knows that she is every bit as determined as Sami in the making-dreams-come-true department!

For a few years now, Alison has been going to night school and taking college classes. That can make for some pretty busy days, considering she's usually at work at 6 A.M.

"My call time is usually between six and six-thirty A.M. We get the blocking for our scenes first, then we tape the show once we get our hair and makeup done. We only get a day [to shoot each] episode," she explains.

So with all that work and studying, how does Ali keep up her energy? Her secret is . . . Diet Coke! "I'll have four or five Diet Cokes a day," she admits. "But then I come to a day when I don't have any, and I'll go into withdrawal. So I'll make myself go for a week without any Diet Coke or caffeine at all. When I'm feeling adventurous I'll go for a Dr Pepper."

Ali has found that her college classes are giving her a unique insight into the world of soap operas. "The classics are often like a soap opera," she explains. "The same thing with Shakespeare. If you think about it, you're talking about a playwright everyone respects, and he basically wrote about the people having affairs with their husband's dead brother, and princes going around pretending they are suicidal—for fun! You get the murder, mayhem, and death. It's really kind of parallel."

Over the years, Sami Brady has gotten herself into some classic Shakespearean trouble, like dating men who are forbidden to her (her sister's boyfriend), and being framed for murder. But the story line that most affected Alison was Sami's teen pregnancy.

"When I would look in the mirror, and I was pregnant, that was really weird," she recalls. "I was so scared. I was like, 'I cannot believe this is happening to me.' It's kind of funny now because I don't think of it as weird anymore, but some days I'll just be like, 'Wow, I'm married, and I have a baby.'"

Having a baby changed Sami's life forever. Working with Shawn and Taylor Carpenter (the twin boys who play baby Will) has changed Alison's as well.

"I learned that I really enjoy being with the babies. But I still don't know what the hard part is like, when you get no sleep and have to change diapers. Nothing can prepare you for that," she says.

Alison really is a big fan of Shawn and Taylor's. She says they are "the sweetest little boys, and they have such outgoing personalities, but when they come on stage, they both get very serious, as though they understand that they have a job to do."

Loving babies is one of the few things sweet Alison has in common with conniving Sami. But there is another characteristic the two have in common—those nails!

"I change [nail polish] colors like every two weeks," Ali says of her salon obsession. "I just have fun being really adventurous with color. I've kind of made them a signature for my character. Sometimes Jeanne Haney (one of the *Days of Our Lives* producers) will tease me about it. She's like, 'Ali, every time you have some crying scene I flinch because your hands come to your face and you have bright green nails!' She always teases me about that."

☆ Nancy Krulik ☆

Sweet Dreams

So what's coming up in Alison's future (besides a new color of nail polish)? For starters, she just bought her own home, and is busy decorating. She's also spending a lot of her precious spare time hanging out with her new boyfriend, Dave.

As for her career, Alison will definitely be spending more days on the *Days of Our Lives* set—she signed a three-year contract last fall. Still, Ali doesn't want to limit her career to playing vicious vixens. She says she'd like to play all kinds of characters. She'd also like to work *behind* the camera someday—directing for TV and film.

But for now, keep your eyes on Alison's Sami Brady. As Alison herself says of Sami, "I'm on the war path again. So LOOK OUT!"

Okay Ali. We're looking! We're looking!

☆ Sizzlin' Soap Stars ☆

☆ Alison Sweeney ☆
Fast Facts

Birthday: September 19
Hair: Blond
Eyes: Blue
Favorite Sports: Kickboxing, horseback riding, swimming, waterskiing, snow skiing, roller blading, basketball, volleyball, and softball (Whew!)
Pets: A gray Thoroughbred horse, Apparition (nicknamed Ghost)
Hobby: Swing dancing

10

Erin Torpey

(Jessica Buchanan, *One Life to Live*)

Erin Torpey would be the first person to tell you that she's just your typical girl-next-door. She's a senior in high school. She's got tons of friends, and she thinks that when she goes to college, she might study psychology. After all, she's the one her friends turn to when they are sad or in need of help. "They all come to me when they have problems," she says. "I always seem to have an answer for them."

Of course to major in college psychology, she'll have to get through math first. And that's not as easy as you may think. "I'm absolutely horrible in math," she confides. "I once flunked algebra and had to take it over. Two of my best friends were in my class so it was even worse, because I never learned anything."

Still, even with studying her math regularly, Erin finds time to drive around in her new Mitsubishi Eclipse Spyder and play pool with friends. And like most seniors she also has a job—it's just that Erin's job gives her a little more pocket money than your average teen. Being a teen soap star does provide you with more than the minimum wage.

But don't kid yourself into believing that Erin's life is full of expensive designer clothing, vacations on the Riviera, and lunches at the Plaza. Nope, when it comes to cash, Erin's a pretty typical teen. Most of the money is being put away—for college.

"The money? I never see it," Erin stresses. "I don't have a credit card, and my mom hardly ever gives me checks. Money? What money?"

Still, Erin knows that she's very lucky to have the kind of job she does.

"I just look at my friends who have to work at McDonalds, and I think, 'Oh my, I'm a lucky girl!'"

The truth is, luck had very little to do with Erin's career. Give the credit to hard work, talent, and perseverance.

Kid, You Oughtta Be in Pictures!

Although Erin has only just turned eighteen, she's actually been in show business longer than some of her older *One Life to Live* costars. She's been a professional actress for more than ten years already!

"When I was really little, I used to sing for

retirement centers. I loved to sing. One day someone told my mother that she should get me a manager," she explains.

Erin's mom, Susan, thought it might be fun for Erin to sing in commercials. And before long, mother and daughter were making regular trips from their Pennsylvania home to New York City for auditions. Lots of kids go to auditions, but they don't all have Erin's success. By the time she was eight, she'd sipped cases of Coke, cuddled Care Bears, munched on Burger King fries, and sung Tiny Tears baby dolls to sleep—all in front of the TV cameras. And if that doesn't impress you, try this one on for size—she was a cast member of Broadway's revival of *Cat on a Hot Tin Roof*, which starred Kathleen Turner and Charles Durning.

Playing opposite such huge stars gave Erin a clear perspective on fame. She discovered that even the most famous actors are just people.

"I didn't even know who Kathleen Turner was back then," Erin admits. "But she was real nice."

Being on Broadway and making commercials isn't always all it's cracked up to be. Imagine being eight years old and working while going to school. You have to memorize your spelling words *and* your script. You're around adults more often than you are around kids your own age. And sometimes you don't know who likes you for *you*, and who just wants to get near a famous star. It's no wonder that many professional kids get so wrapped up in their careers that they can't relate to their peers.

But that's not Erin's story at all. "I had such a normal life," Erin recalls. "I'd go for auditions after school, and if I had a field trip I wouldn't go [to the audition]. If I had a birthday party to go to I either wouldn't go to the audition, or I'd be home in time to make it to at least some of the party. My parents were so good about that."

But Erin recalls meeting kids whose parents were not so good about it. And those kids developed into real Broadway brats. "I'd go to auditions and the kids were so mean," Erin explains. "They wouldn't want to play. I'd try to become friends with whoever I could, waiting to audition or backstage, but the kids were such brats. I liked going home and being normal. I didn't want to be like those kids."

Relax Erin, you're about as far from being a brat as you can be!

Welcome to Llanview

In 1991, Erin found herself on the set of *One Life to Live*. She'd been cast as Clint and Viki's daughter, Jessica. The character of Jessica was nine years old when Erin took over the role, and already she'd been kidnapped by an ex–cult member who had burned down the family home.

☆ Nancy Krulik ☆

Jessica was a regular character on *One Life to Live*, but that didn't mean Erin had to give up her own life to play her. "In the beginning I worked once every two weeks, if that," Erin explained. "The show was just an hour away in New York. So I could still go to school."

Even though she spent very little time on the set, Erin developed close ties with her TV family. Erika Slezak, who plays Jessica's mom on the show, became like a second mother to Erin. In fact Erin recalls that when she got her first car she was five weeks too young to drive it. Her mother drove her into the city to show the car off to her coworkers. When Erin and her real mom arrived at the parking lot, Erin's TV mom had just pulled in. Erika's son Michael jumped into the new car with Erin. Then, Erin's real mom and her TV mom both started snapping pictures of the two teens smiling happily in Erin's first car.

Besides her personal closeness to her TV family, Erin is grateful for the opportunity to work beside them. "I learn so much from Erika," she says gratefully. "I learn so much from all of them."

Erin Gets a *HOT* New Leading Man

As the years went on, the character of Jessica began to take on a larger role in the Buchanan family. Although the character came from a wealthy family, the sheltered teen got herself involved with the Angel Square gang. She also started a true romance with Cristian Vega.

The more Jessica's story lines became intertwined with those of the rest of the *One Life to Live* cast, the longer the hours Erin had to work. That meant that sometimes Erin had to pass on going to the mall with her friends, or going to a party the night before an early-morning call.

Still, disappointments like that are easy to take when you have to look your best for a luscious leading man like *One Life to Live*'s David Fumero. In the summer of 1998, the hot Cuban-born model was brought in to replace Yorlin Madera as Cristian. David was already famous as a model for Giorgio Armani. He was also several years older than Erin, and that made her nervous.

"David is just adorable," Erin admitted to *Soap Opera Digest*. "There is a little problem though. David's a bit older. He was probably, 'Oh my God. I have to kiss this girl!'"

But Erin had nothing to fear. As David told *Soap Opera Digest* last summer, "Erin's a great girl. It's been nice working with her."

Erin wasn't the only one made nervous by David's entrance on to the show. When Erin became sick in the middle of the summer and had to be replaced temporarily by a slightly older actress, fans became concerned that the show was looking to replace her with an actress more in David's age range. But they didn't need to worry. The show simply needed someone to fill in while Erin was recuperating. Jessica's story line was just too important to let it dangle while her portrayer was ill. The producers had no plans to replace Erin permanently. She returned to the show two weeks after she took her sick leave.

Actually *David* was the one with real reason to fear. He was the newcomer. Erin had grown up on the set. Everyone in Llanview feels very protective of her. "It's funny, because when I do a kissing scene, the whole time, Alan, our stage manager, goes, 'I'll kill him. I'll kill him if he kisses you!'" Erin says with a laugh.

It's a good thing David's grandfather taught him some self-defense techniques before the boy left Cuba.

"My grandfather sat me and my brothers down and taught us how to box and gave us lessons on how to become men," David says. "He told us we were kids but we had to behave like men and be strong. I'll never forget those words."

The addition of David Fumero to the cast of *One Life to Live* came not too long after the show hired two of the most talented soap opera writers around—Claire and Matthew Labine. They are the ones who created the famous Robin and Stone story line on *General Hospital*—the one in which Stone not only contracted and died from AIDS, but unknowingly gave it to his teenager lover, Robin Scorpio. The Robin/Stone story line helped Kimberly McCullough (GH's Robin) win a daytime Emmy award, and Erin is not shy in saying that she hopes Claire and Matthew can give her a story that is every bit as juicy.

"Already I can see that their writing is very realistic—especially for me on a teenage level," Erin says.

Claire and Matthew have made Jessica's role more intense, and given her an even larger presence on the show. Her relationship with Cristian has been jeopardized by Roseanne, a beautiful model who has been his muse for his new paintings. Jessica's insecurities have driven her and her stepbrother Will into several bad experiences, including an arrest and a one-night stand which led to Jessica becoming pregnant.

Erin is very excited about the twists and turns Jessica's life has taken. "It's fun," she says. "When I was little, I had nothing. Now, it's kind of like my own life. More fun and more interesting."

And more time consuming. In fact, last summer, Erin was on the set so many days that she had to move to New York for a few weeks—on her own! Well, sort of on her own. Although her real mom and dad stayed back in Pennsylvania, her TV family was watching out for her. She stayed in an apartment that belongs to Robin Strasser (Dorian on *One Life to Live*). It was a two-bedroom apartment. Erin stayed in one room, and Robin would come by to use the other room for work. So although Erin was there alone, Robin was checking in.

And just to keep on the safe side, Erin's mom checked in a lot, too. "Oh my God," Erin laughs. "You don't even know. My mom called every night!"

Well Erin, moms will be moms.

Erin's new TV exposure has been a hard adjustment for her real-life boyfriend. "He knows I have to kiss and stuff like that, but it's not all that easy for him. So when I go home I just try not to talk about it."

Still, as normal as Erin is, there's no mistaking that she's a star. When she and her friends are out, fans will sometimes come up to her. They feel as though they know her. After all, she did grow up in their living rooms.

"Everyone says, 'Oh my gosh, I've known you since you were this big,'" she explains. "That's kind of scary. When fans come up to me, I

☆ Sizzlin' Soap Stars ☆

sometimes get weird. I don't mind it, but I don't know what to say."

Well, you'd better get working on that witty repartee, Erin, because as Jessica's life becomes more complicated, more fans than ever are going to want to meet their favorite Buchanan up close and personal.

☆ Erin Torpey ☆
Fast Facts

Birthday: February 14
Hair: Blond
Eyes: Blue
Siblings: An older sister, Shannon
Favorite singers: Sarah McLachlan and Jewel
Favorite Sports: Roller blading, tennis, swimming
Hobby: Talking on the phone (See, she really is a typical teen!)
Favorite TV Show: MTV's *The Real World*

11

Jacob Young

(Rick Forrester, *The Bold and the Beautiful*)

Imagine walking off the stage from your small-town high school play and going directly to the soundstage of a hit TV show. Sounds like something that could only happen on the soaps, right? Well, surprise! That's pretty much how it happened in real life for Jacob Young, the latest in a long line of bold and beautiful men to star on the most watched TV show in the world, *The Bold and the Beautiful*.

"I was right out of high school when I decided I wanted to pursue acting full-time. It happened that it hit quick," Jacob explains. "I started the show [in January 1998] as soon as I decided to get into the industry. Bell-Phillip, the production company, saw an ad that I had placed in a magazine [*Variety Junior*, a version of *Daily Variety*] and they called me into casting. I ended up beating out some 250 men for the role."

One person involved with the casting for the

role of Rick Forrester was Jacob's costar, Adrienne Frantz (Amber). Since Adrienne would be playing a lot of intimate scenes with the actor chosen for the role, it was important that she felt comfortable with her costar. "There was something about him," Adrienne says. "I just knew he was the one."

Adrienne was right. The chemistry between Amber and Rick has been electric! In fact it's so hot that *TV Guide* recently praised Jacob, Adrienne, and their costar Mick Cain (C. J.), saying that "*B&B*'s teens are a gas!" The magazine specifically praised Jacob and Mick, predicting that the actors are "both destined for major careers!"

Whew! That's high praise for a kid whose previous resume only included roles in high school productions of *Grease, Guys and Dolls, The Wizard of Oz,* and *Our Town.*

But Jacob is handling his newfound fame with ease. When fans recognize him on the street, he never pulls a "star trip"—even when they call him Rick instead of Jacob.

"Most people are nice; they just praise you. And they only know you as your character, which is *interesting*," he admits. "While I enjoyed my life before the show, when people didn't know who I was, I definitely enjoy being who I am today. It's exactly what I had hoped."

And when fans get angry, criticizing Jacob for the things Rick has done, Jacob acknowledges their feelings without ever getting angry. As he told one on-line critic, "I don't always like it either. But I don't write the scripts. I have to take what's given and do my best with it. I never know what Rick is going to do."

Jacob has obviously learned to handle critics. But that kind of diplomacy has always come easily to the youngest member of the Young family.

Before Stardom

Jacob Young was born in the small town of Renton, Washington. He's the youngest of four children. (He has two older sisters and an older brother.) The family soon moved to Tillamook, Oregon, a place Jacob describes as "where the cheddar is made."

Jacob was different than most of the kids he knew growing up. For one thing, he discovered acting when he was thirteen, and by the time he was fifteen he was onstage in high school productions. In his first show, *Grease*, he played one of the dancers in the chorus. It wasn't a leading role, but as folks in the biz say, there are no small parts, only small actors. The theater bug had bitten Jacob—hard! He knew from then on what his passion was.

"I'm the only one in my family who pursued acting," Jacob explains, "but that's definitely an inspiration to myself, that I'm just being my own person and doing my own thing."

And doing his own thing meant hanging out with several different cliques in high school. Besides being part of the theater crowd, Jacob was also a wrestler, ranking nationally in freestyle and Greco-Roman–style wrestling. Still, with all those achievements, he says he wasn't exactly the Big Man on Campus in high school.

"I wasn't real popular when I was in high school," he admits. "But now I'm the hometown hero, and very popular when I go home."

Of course, not all of his friends at home are new. In fact, Jacob says he depends on his old high school buddies to keep him grounded.

"They give you the reality check," he says. "Because they were there before, you can trust them. It's the friends [you get] after you find fame that you have to be wary of."

Jacob's pals say he hasn't changed much as a result of his overnight success. In fact, although he admits to being shocked at the size of his first few *Bold and the Beautiful* paychecks ("I sure didn't make that much at Denny's," he jokes), Jacob hasn't made any major purchases other than his new dream car, a beautiful BMW silver roadster. But Jacob must not be completely comfortable in his new pricey car, because he's usually seen driving around in a 1963 Volkswagen Beetle he restored while he was in high school.

Jacob's family provides him with a wonderful support system. Although his closest family members are in Oregon, he talks to them regularly by phone. Jacob swears his mom is his biggest fan. (Although there are plenty of women out there who are fighting her for that title!) Jacob's grandparents are also excited about his soap opera success, although they have a few problems with some of his steamy love scenes.

"Whenever Rick's love scenes come on, they switch the channel," Jacob told *Soap Opera Weekly*. "I think they do that because they are not really used to seeing their grandson as someone who is in a romantic relationship. They'll wait a few minutes and then turn right back to the show."

Jacob's grandparents had better keep that remote handy. Last summer's love triangle between Rick, Amber, and Raymond (played by red-hot rapper Usher) took center stage. Obviously audiences want to see more romance from Rick!

Life on the Set

When Jacob first took on the role of Rick, the character had a long legacy as the son of Brooke and Eric Forrester, two of *The Bold and the Beautiful*'s most beloved characters. As is the case with so many soap opera offspring, the character of Rick was aged quickly, so that more spicy teenage story lines could be added to *The Bold and the Beautiful*'s already thick soup of love, lust, and treachery. Jacob spent a lot of his first few months on the job researching Rick's past history. "It was difficult," Jacob admits, "but I adjusted."

Another adjustment was remembering how to be sixteen again. When Jacob took over the role of Rick he was already eighteen. "I have to look back on how I was when I was that age . . . how I lived through that time and experienced it," Jacob explains.

One thing Jacob still hasn't become accustomed to is the huge amount of lines he has to memorize each night. "The biggest challenge is memorization," he admits. "There's anywhere from eight to thirty pages of dialogue a day. We have no cue cards or teleprompter so everything has to be memorized. It's very difficult, but the more you do it, the easier it becomes."

To help him memorize, Jacob uses some of his old high school tricks. For starters, he always does his studying in the same place—a small corner of his apartment. And he doesn't keep lots of things around that might distract him from his memorizing. The only things he keeps in his study cubby-

☆ Sizzlin' Soap Stars ☆

hole are a lamp and a photo of his idol, fifties movie actor James Dean. Jacob told *Soap Opera Digest* that he sometimes feels like the late actor's spirit is with him while he does his work.

Whatever the reason, the character of Rick is becoming more and more of a rebel—something that James Dean, star of the classic flick *Rebel Without a Cause*, would have loved. Viewers of *B&B* might notice that Rick's look has become more rebellious since his affair with Amber began.

"When a character joins the show, I'll talk to the producers and writers to see what look they want," *B&B*'s costume designer Laurie Robinson explained to *Soap Opera Magazine*. "Rick started out with a vintage '50s look, but as he's grown rebellious, we've gone with some darker tones."

And Jacob is enjoying the acting challenges his character's darker personality provides him with.

"At first the character was very out of it, sheltered," he explains. "Now he's experiencing more grown-up things. He's taking charge, standing up for himself."

When he's on the set, Jacob hangs out mostly with Adrienne and Mick. They pal around on Stage 31 of CBS Television City (where *B&B* is shot), spending time in Adrienne's dressing room (it's the closest to the set) watching the *Jerry Springer Show*.

Unfortunately, with ten- or eleven-hour days on

the set, and plenty of lines to memorize before the next day's 8:30 A.M. call, Jacob, Adrienne, and Mick don't find much time to socialize off the set. Jacob tends to spend what little free time he has horseback riding and surfing.

Surfing is a newfound passion for Jacob. "[Surfing] can be scary," he admits. "From the start you've got to learn to appreciate the water, recognize that it's a mighty force and respect it. Don't ever take it for granted, because as soon as you do, the seas will take you for your final ride. There's a little danger that does appeal to me. It's definitely a thrill."

And riding the waves isn't the only thing Jacob likes about living in California. "I'm finding it very appealing," he says of L.A. "I'm meeting all sorts of interesting new people, discovering wonderful new restaurants. It has really enlightened me in so many ways."

Some of those interesting new people Jacob's meeting are women, naturally. And while meeting up with some of L.A.'s more beautiful ladies is great, Jacob says that where women are concerned, he definitely goes for "personality first, and looks second." He adds, "For me, it's always been family first. And I guess, one day, when the time is right, I'll have a family of my own."

☆ Sizzlin' Soap Stars ☆

Looking to the Future

Like most soap stars, Jacob finds the challenges of daily tapings and character intrigue a wonderful opportunity for learning. He eagerly admits that *The Bold and the Beautiful* is the best training ground there is. But ask Jacob where he sees himself in ten years, and he's liable to tell you, "Hopefully by then I will have expanded into feature films. And I'll have a very productive career in it."

He also yearns for the Great White Way. "I will definitely be shooting for Broadway some time in the future," he says. "That would be a realistic goal."

Whatever route Jacob decides to take in his future career, one thing is certain: his fans will remain loyal. After all, it's not often that a star is as bold and beautiful on the inside as he is on the outside.

☆ Jacob Young ☆
Fast Facts

Birthday: September 10
Hair: Blond
Eyes: Sky blue
Height: 5'10"
Favorite Sport: Race car driving
Hobbies: Surfing, horseback riding, hanging out with friends
Favorite Movies: *East of Eden, Giant, Rebel Without a Cause* (all three star James Dean)
Favorite TV Shows: *Spin City, Seinfeld* reruns
Actress He'd Most Like to Meet: Cameron Diaz
People He Most Admires: "My parents, for putting up with me all these years!"

The Ultimate Soap Opera Trivia Quiz

Okay, so now you know all you need to know about today's hottest rising soap stars. But just how much do you know about the shows they appear on?

There's just one way to find out. Put down your remote control and pick up a pencil. It's time to take a daring daytime drama quiz. There are questions about every soap on the air today. We're gonna separate the daytime dilettantes from the true soap opera addicts! Stay tuned. Here come the questions!

All My Children
Premiere Date: 1/5/70

1. Why did Erica Kane once go to jail?
2. Name Erica's anorexic daughter.

3. Where does *All My Children* take place?
4. At what big event did Trevor first propose to Janet?
5. Name the show hosted by Tad Martin.
6. Who is Adam Chandler's twin brother?
7. Who was Erica's first husband?
8. When Janet's ex-husband refused to return, what did she do to deceive Trevor?
9. Brooke is editor in chief of what magazine?
10. Who kidnapped Hayley and Adam Chandler Jr., threatening to make them pay for the sins of Adam Chandler Sr.?
11. What food chain does Palmer Cortlandt own?
12. Which *All My Children* character had frightening visions which predicted the future?
13. Who is the natural father of Liza's baby—Jake or Adam?
14. Why did Gillian marry Ryan?
15. Who runs the boarding house?

☆ Sizzlin' Soap Stars ☆

Answers to the *All My Children* Quiz

1. For kidnapping baby Sonya
2. Bianca
3. Pine Valley
4. At the Crystal Ball
5. *The Cutting Edge*
6. Stuart Chandler
7. She eloped with med student Jeff Martin in 1971.
8. She hired an actor to play Axel.
9. *Tempo*
10. Lee Hawkins
11. Cluck Cluck Chicken
12. Mateo
13. Because of a mix-up at the fertility clinic, Adam is the father.
14. She married him so she would not be deported.
15. Myrtle Fargate

Another World
Premiere Date: 5/4/64

1. Name the publishing house where Amanda works.
2. In what fictional city does *Another World* take place?

3. The night before her marriage to Jake, Vicky got trapped somewhere with Shane. Where?
4. Gary Sinclair is recovering from what problem?
5. Who is Lorna's and Jenna's mother?
6. Who once saved Nicole from being run over by a truck?
7. Who is Vicky's twin sister?
8. What did Vicky give Marley in an attempt to save her life?
9. What conniving schemer landed herself a job as Felicia's secretary?
10. Whose real name is Fanny Grady?
11. What *Another World* star is also a jazz singer who takes time off to perform with her husband, Rodney Kendrick?
12. What famous movie actress once played Vicky?
13. Who is the real father of Lila's baby?
14. True or false: Before marrying Jake, Paulina tried to kill him.
15. What restaurant does Sofia's brother Joe own?

☆ Sizzlin' Soap Stars ☆

Answers to the *Another World* Quiz

1. Cory Publishing
2. Bay City
3. On a boat
4. Alcoholism
5. Felicia Gallant
6. Cass
7. Marley
8. Bone marrow
9. Remy
10. Felicia Gallant
11. Rhonda Ross Kendrick (She's also the daughter of Diana Ross.)
12. Ann Heche
13. Matt
14. True
15. Carlino's

As The World Turns
Premiere Date: 4/2/56

1. Where did Lily go to find out about her past after discovering she was adopted?
2. Who was pronounced dead after a plane crash, but was really hiding in a monastery?
3. What TV show does Kim host?

4. Who owns the Mona Lisa restaurant and the *Argus* newspaper?
5. Who did Lily meet in prison?
6. What does Margo do for a living?
7. Who almost killed Margo in the school yard?
8. Who is Luke's mother?
9. Where does *As the World Turns* take place?
10. Why did David kidnap Lily?
11. Who killed Eddie's mother, Deena?
12. Who was married to Margo, Carol, and Natalie, and once was engaged to Barbara?
13. Mary Ellen Walters is also known as whom?
14. What does Barbara Ryan do?
15. Who is Margo's younger sister?

Answers to the *As the World Turns* Quiz

1. Wyoming
2. Damian
3. *Patterns*
4. Lisa Grimaldi
5. Molly
6. She's a police officer.

☆ Sizzlin' Soap Stars ☆

7. Chuck—he took her gun and threatened to kill her. Eddie came by and saved her life.
8. Lily
9. Oakdale
10. To steal her baby, Lucinda's grandchild. He wanted to get back at Lucinda for trying to run him out of town.
11. Margo killed her during a drug bust.
12. Tom
13. Lucinda Walsh
14. She's a fashion designer.
15. Katie

The Bold and the Beautiful
Premiere Date: 3/23/87

1. Who were the two possible fathers of Amber's baby?
2. Ridge is the lead designer for what fashion firm?
3. True or false: Maggie was once in love with her daughter Jessica's boyfriend.
4. Name the CEO of Spectra.
5. Who was the surrogate mother of James and Maggie's baby?
6. Which of Eric and Stephanie's sons married both Brooke and Taylor?

7. True or false: Brooke once had a nervous breakdown.
8. What disease did Grant have?
9. True or false: Brooke avoided going to Ridge's wedding to Taylor by flying to Paris on the Concorde.
10. Why was Sheila sentenced to a term in the mental hospital?
11. Who traded identities with Sheila so Sheila could escape from the mental hospital?
12. C. J. suggested Amber give up her baby for adoption. Who did he suggest she give the baby to?
13. Who did Maggie Forrester once kidnap?
14. Amber is a nickname for _____.
15. Who is C. J.'s real father?

Answers to the *Bold and the Beautiful* Quiz

1. Rick and Raymond
2. House of Forrester Fashions
3. True. His name was Dylan.
4. Sally Spectra
5. Sheila
6. Ridge
7. True

☆ Sizzlin' Soap Stars ☆

8. Cancer
9. False. In fact she went to the wedding, in the hopes that he would not go through with it.
10. For threatening baby Thomas's life
11. Sybil
12. Macy
13. Sheila
14. Ambrosia
15. Clarke

Days of Our Lives
Premiere Date: 11/8/65

1. Who is the son of murderer Curtis Reed and Kate Roberts?
2. Who is Sami's twin brother?
3. True or false: Kate was once a prostitute.
4. Is Austin Will's father?
5. Bo has a tattoo he got in Stockholm. What is it a picture of?
6. In what city does *Days Of Our Lives* take place?
7. What is Marlena's profession?
8. Who gave Bo back his eyesight after he was attacked by bats?
9. Who did Sami dress as to celebrate Franco's birthday?

10. Which *DOOL* character was once possessed by the devil?
11. Who is Nicole's sister?
12. What is the name of the bar owned by Roman's father, Shawn?
13. How did Sami once develop amnesia?
14. What does Mickey do for a living?
15. Who did Kate hire to come between Hope and Bo?

Answers to the *Days of Our Lives* Quiz

1. Austin
2. Eric
3. True
4. No. Lucas is his natural father.
5. A dagger
6. Salem
7. She's a psychiatrist.
8. Swamp Girl
9. Marilyn Monroe
10. Marlena
11. Taylor
12. Brady's Pub
13. She was hit by a car.
14. He's a district attorney.
15. Franco

☆ Sizzlin' Soap Stars ☆

General Hospital
Premiere Date: 4/1/63

1. What is Lucky Spencer's full name?
2. True or false: Mac is Georgie's father.
3. What *Full House* dad played Blackie Parrish on GH in the 1980s?
4. What is Jax's real first name?
5. Robin Scorpio's late father, Robert, once worked for the WSB. What did those letters stand for?
6. What did Robin's lover Stone die from?
7. What did Emily Quartermaine's mother die from?
8. Who was driving the car that slammed into a tree, giving Jason life-altering brain damage?
9. Who is Eddie Maine?
10. Who saved Lesley Lu's life?
11. Who is Bobbie's long-lost daughter?
12. Who is Michael's natural father?
13. Who is Nikolas's real father?
14. Name the restaurant Mac opened.
15. Who left Brenda at the altar?

☆ Nancy Krulik ☆

Answers to the *General Hospital* Quiz

1. Lucas Lorenzo Spencer Jr.
2. False. Felicia's former husband, Frisco, is.
3. John Stamos
4. Jasper
5. World Security Bureau
6. AIDS
7. Breast cancer
8. A. J.
9. Ned Ashton's alias when he performed music secretly
10. Nikolas. He donated his bone marrow to save her.
11. Carly
12. A. J.
13. Stefan Cassidine
14. The Outback
15. Sonny

Guiding Light
Premiere Dates: 1/37 (on radio),
6/30/52 (on television)

1. How long was each episode of *Guiding Light* when it first began on radio?
   a. 15 minutes   b. 30 minutes   c. 60 minutes

☆ Sizzlin' Soap Stars ☆

2. What footloose movie star once played teen alcoholic Tim Werner?
3. What do Darth Vader and *Guiding Light*'s Dr. Jim Frazier have in common?
4. Who did *Beverly Hills 90210* star Ian Ziering once play on *Guiding Light*?
5. Where does *Guiding Light* take place?
6. Name the drug Roger used to poison Dinah.
7. What was the name of Reva's clone?
8. How did the clone die?
9. An accident left Michelle temporarily afflicted with what handicap?
10. Who has Maureen's heart?
11. What poisoned fruit did Harley bite into?
12. Who runs WSPR?
13. What crime did Abigail commit?
14. What book did Phillip Spaulding author?
15. What *Guiding Light* character was born in an Amish community?

Answers to the *Guiding Light* Quiz

1. a
2. Kevin Bacon
3. Both were played by James Earl Jones.
4. Cameron Stewart

☆ Nancy Krulik ☆

5. Springfield
6. Lonotrat
7. Dolly
8. She took growth serum.
9. She was blinded.
10. Paolo—he got it through a transplant.
11. An apple
12. Dinah
13. She murdered Roy Meachum, although she was soon released from jail when the murder was called justifiable.
14. *Zanzibar*
15. Abigail

One Life to Live
Premiere Date: 7/15/68

1. What is the *Banner*?
2. What kind of illness did Viki once suffer from?
3. Who is the owner of the *Intruder*?
4. Which of Max's children is deaf?
   a. Al   b. Lesley   c. Frankie
5. Which of Asa's ex-wives owns the Palace Hotel?
6. What does Cristian do for a living?
7. What is the name of Todd's pet parrot?
8. What type of business does R. J. run?

☆ Sizzlin' Soap Stars ☆

9. What name did Todd give to his faked alternate personality?
10. Who was Jessica with when she was arrested?
11. Who murdered Georgie?
12. After Viki decided to remarry Clint, what did she discover he had done with Lindsey?
13. Who are Starr's parents?
14. Viki's son Kevin was once injured in a fire at Llanfair. What did he have to learn to do again while he was recuperating?
15. Which of Viki's children once set the family home on fire?

Answers to the *One Life to Life* Quiz

1. A Llanview newspaper
2. Multiple personalities
3. Dorian
4. c
5. Renee
6. He's a painter.
7. Moose
8. A record company
9. Tom
10. Will

11. Rachel
12. He married her in Las Vegas.
13. Todd and Tea
14. Walk
15. Jessica

Port Charles
Premiere Date: 6/1/97

1. What San Francisco policeman was Karen once married to?
2. Which disgruntled intern shot Audrey Hardy?
3. What construction tool did Joe Scanlon use to operate on Audrey?
4. At Lucy and Kevin's double wedding with Mac and Felicia, only one couple married. Who was that couple?
5. When Greg Cooper kidnapped Julie and held her captive in the basement of his family home, what did he threaten to do to her?
6. Who did Lucy once marry simply to protect Serena?
7. Who poisoned Lucy?
8. Who is the author of *General Homicide*?
9. Name the drug that made Frank angry and violent.

☆ Sizzlin' Soap Stars ☆

10. What did Serena lose in her car accident?
11. Lucy once rescued Ellen from what type of animal?
12. Name Lucy's duck.
13. Who is the resident in charge of the interns?
14. Name Scotty Baldwin's wives.
15. Name Kevin's dead evil identical twin.

Answers to the *Port Charles* Quiz

1. Jagger Cates
2. Greg Cooper
3. A power drill
4. Mac and Felicia
5. He threatened to perform hideous plastic surgery on her face.
6. Rex
7. Rex
8. Kevin
9. DL56
10. Her eyesight
11. A bear
12. Sigmund
13. Dr. Ellen Burgess
14. Laura Webber Spencer, Susan Moore, and Dominique Taub
15. Ryan Chamberlain

Sunset Beach
Premiere Date: 1/6/97

1. Upon her arrival in Sunset Beach, Melinda fell off the pier and into whose arms?
2. Caitlin once fell off a cliff, but she didn't die—where did she wind up instead?
3. What disease did Doc Tyus and Michael believe Vanessa suffered from?
4. What landlocked state does Sara come from?
5. Who did Ben push off a cliff?
6. What does Casey do for a living?
7. Where had Melinda originally met Sara?
8. True or false: Alex is in remission from cancer.
9. Bette Katzenkazrahi is whose aunt?
10. Name the coffee house owned by Ben.
11. Caitlin was not really pregnant at her wedding to Cole. What slip up almost revealed her secret?
12. Who is the real mother of Caitlin's baby?
13. What does Gregory do for a living?
14. Name the cruise ship that capsized when it was hit by a tsunami.
15. Where did Casey and Sara wind up after the shipwreck?

☆ Sizzlin' Soap Stars ☆

Answers to the *Sunset Beach* Quiz

1. Casey's
2. In a convent
3. Martin's Syndrome
4. Kansas
5. His crazed brother, Derek
6. He's a lifeguard.
7. Washington, D.C.
8. True
9. Annie's
10. Java Web
11. The padded fake pregnant stomach slipped out from beneath her wedding gown.
12. Olivia, who is also Caitlin's mother
13. He's an attorney.
14. SS *Neptune*
15. On a deserted island

The Young and the Restless
Premiere Date: 3/26/83

1. Sharon was once surprised to discover that Cassie was really whom?
2. Psychotic lawyer Michael Baldwin wants to destroy someone. Who?
   a. Jack   b. Christine   c. Nikki

3. When *The Young and the Restless* first premiered, it focused on the loves and lives of what family?
4. Name Victor and Nikki's children.
5. What *Baywatch* star once played Snapper on *The Young and the Restless*?
6. What real-life actress had a face-lift at the same time her character did?
7. True or false: Nina once went crazy and shot Ryan.
8. Where did Jack first meet his late wife, Luann?
9. What does Malcolm do for a living?
10. Where does *The Young and the Restless* take place?
11. Ryan married Victoria because he thought he would someday be the head of what?
12. Who is Bern Bennett?
13. What is the name of Malcolm's dead wife?
14. What product does the Jabot company make?
15. Who are Noah's parents?

Answers to the *Young and the Restless* Quiz

1. Her long lost daughter
2. b

☆ Sizzlin' Soap Stars ☆

3. The Brooks family
4. Victoria and Nicholas
5. David Hasselhoff
6. Jeanne Cooper (Katherine)
7. False. She shot herself.
8. Viet Nam
9. He's a photographer.
10. Genoa City
11. Newman Enterprises
12. The show's announcer
13. Keesha
14. Cosmetics
15. Sharon and Nick

Roll Credits!

Now that you've demonstrated your amazing knowledge about soap opera paternity tests, illicit affairs, cases of amnesia, secret murders, and mob bosses with hearts of gold, it's time to find out how you stack up against other super suds fans. To check your score, give yourself credit for each of your correct answers. Then check the chart below. There are 165 possible correct answers.

150–165 correct: Wow! You must must spend all the days of your life watching the soaps. You should get out more—you only have one life to live, you know.

100–149 correct: A fantastic score. Have you got a clone like Reva's to do some of that watching for you?

☆ Sizzlin' Soap Stars ☆

75–99 correct: You are a true soap fan. You know, the kind that fantasizes about buying Barbara Ryan fashions at Wyndhams Department Store, while watching Erica Kane model.

45–74 correct: Ooh. Those soap bubbles seem to be popping quickly. But before you start feeling like Susan Lucci at the Emmy Awards, chill out. All you have to do to bring up your score is turn on the tube and settle in for a few good hours.

0–44 correct: Has your VCR been out of order? It seems like you haven't seen a soap in a long, long time. But don't worry, you can catch up on what's been happening, and you won't even have to tune in tomorrow. Just reread this book, and try the quiz again!

About the Author

When NANCY KRULIK isn't watching soaps (she's partial to *General Hospital* and *Days of Our Lives*), she is busy writing celebrity biographies of stars like Leonardo DiCaprio, Taylor Hanson, and 'N Sync's JC Chasez. She's also the author of *Pop Quiz*, a music trivia book, and *Pop Quiz: Leonardo DiCaprio*. She lives in Manhattan with her husband, composer Daniel Burwasser, and their two children.

Think you know everything about today's hottest heartthrob, Leonardo DiCaprio? It's time to take the *ultimate* test of Leo trivia and see if you're truly his number-one fan!

Quiz:
Leonardo DiCaprio

Nancy Krulik

With a special fold-out poster of Leo!

From Archway Paperback
Published by Pocket Books

THE HOTTEST STARS THE BEST BIOGRAPHIES

☆ **Hanson: MMMBop to the Top** ☆
By Jill Mattthews

☆ **Hanson: The Ultimate Trivia Book!** ☆
By Matt Netter

☆ **Isaac Hanson: Totally Ike!** ☆
By Nancy Krulik

☆ **Taylor Hanson: Totally Taylor!** ☆
By Nancy Krulik

☆ **Zac Hanson: Totally Zac!** ☆
By Matt Netter

☆ **Jonathan Taylor Thomas: Totally JTT!** ☆
By Michael-Anne Johns

☆ **Leonardo DiCaprio: A Biography** ☆
By Nancy Krulik

☆ **Will Power! A Biography of Will Smith** ☆
By Jan Berenson

☆ **Prince William: The Boy Who Will Be King** ☆
By Randi Reisfeld

Available from Archway Paperbacks
Published by Pocket Books

1491

What's it like to be a Witch?

Sabrina The Teenage Witch

"I'm 16, I'm a Witch and I still have to go to school!"

♦♦♦♦♦

#1 Sabrina, the Teenage Witch
#2 Showdown at the Mall
#3 Good Switch, Bad Switch
#4 Halloween Havoc
#5 Santa's Little Helper
#6 Ben There, Done That
#7 All You Need is a Love Spell
#8 Salem on Trial
#9 A Dog's Life
#10 Lotsa Luck
#11 Prisoner of Cabin 13
#12 All That Glitters
#13 Go Fetch
#14 Spying Eyes
Sabrina Goes to Rome
#15 Harvest Moon
#16 Now You See Her, Now You Don't
#17 Eight Spells A Week
#18 I'll Zap Manhattan
#19 Shamrock Shenanigans
#20 Age of Aquariums
#21 Prom Time
#22 Witchopoly

Based on the hit TV series
Look for a new title every other month.

From Archway Paperbacks
Published by Pocket Books

1345-10

No mission is ever impossible!

Join the

on all of their supercool missions
as they jet-set around the world
in search of truth and justice!

The secret is out! Read

**LICENSE TO THRILL
LIVE AND LET SPY
NOBODY DOES IT BETTER
SPY GIRLS ARE FOREVER**

 Available from Archway Paperbacks